CLASSIC
CHINESE
CUISINE

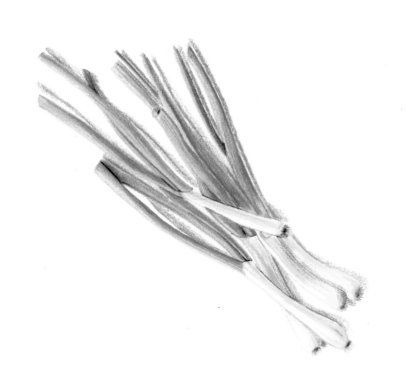

Classic Chinese Cuisine

Kenneth Lo

SIMON & SCHUSTER

LONDON·SYDNEY·NEW YORK·TOKYO·SINGAPORE·TORONTO

First published in Great Britain by
Simon & Schuster Ltd in 1992
A Paramount Communications Company

Copyright © In the text: Kenneth Lo
          © Illustrations: Helen Semmler

This book is copyright under the Berne Convention.
No reproduction without permission.
All rights reserved.

Simon & Schuster Ltd
West Garden Place
Kendal Street
London W2 2AQ

Simon & Schuster of Australia Pty Ltd
Sydney

A CIP catalogue record for this book is
available from the British Library
ISBN 0-671-71161-X

Designed and illustrated by Helen Semmler
Typeset in Australia by Asset Typesetting Pty Ltd
Printed in Hong Kong by South China Printing Co. Ltd

CONTENTS

INTRODUCTION

ONE OF THE MOST remarkable things about China is that even though it has a population of over a billion people, the majority are reasonably well fed. This has been possible only because of intensive labour, a decentralized economy, and flexible use and cultivation of agricultural products. In the north and north-west, people cultivate and consume wheat, corn and maize. Along the Yangzi (Yangtze) River, the main agricultural produce is rice, which is produced in three crops a year in the southern semi-tropical provinces such as Guangdong (Kwangtung). In the mountainous areas of the coastal south-east, sweet potatoes are grown to supplement the rice.

For the average Chinese family meal, these cereals are supplemented by meat, poultry, fish and seafood, and vegetables. The meat and seafood supplements are used as flavourers, with good Chinese meals consisting of large quantities of vegetables and rice, and a little meat. A home-cooked Chinese meal can be both extremely economical and healthy.

A few years ago I wrote a book entitled *Cheap Chow* (in the United States of America it was called *Chinese Cooking on Next to Nothing*). When it was launched in London by my publisher, we threw a party, which was attended by nearly 100 journalists, where the Chinese food served was limited to a total cost of UK £15 (A$37/US$30).

While some very appetizing and nourishing dishes can be cheap, one should be aware, however, that some Chinese meals can also be among the most expensive in the world. This may be because the ingredients can only be harvested in small quantities or require a lot of preparation. Recently an American magazine, the *Smithsonian*, researched that the top grade bird's-nest was valued at US$600 per ounce

(A$27 per gram/UK£300 per ounce) — slightly dearer than gold! Hence Chinese food is one of the very few classical cuisines of the world which can be served in affluent countries as well as in impoverished nations.

What then are the top 100 Chinese dishes? They are certainly neither the most expensive, nor the cheapest. They can only be the dishes that reflect the "Good Earth" of China — those which are meaningful to eat and reminiscent of the flavour of life and food in China. At the same time, such dishes should also possess universal appeal if they are to be accepted by the rest of the world.

With this loose definition as my guideline, I have brought together my favourite and the most popular Chinese dishes I have encountered, both in China and abroad, in over three-quarters of a century — the time that I have been eating Chinese food!

Please note: the tablespoon measurements used in this book are equivalent to the UK and US standards of 15 mL or 3 teaspoons. The Australian standard tablespoon measures 20 mL or 4 teaspoons.

THE CHINESE KITCHEN

THE CHINESE KITCHEN

NO MORE THAN two or three decades ago, most of the cooking in China was done on wood, charcoal, or coal fires. Nowadays, the Chinese kitchen is growing to resemble that of the Western kitchen — most urban cooking is done on gas — however, it is still much more simply equipped. We employ far fewer gadgets: hardly any kitchen would contain a blender or a microwave oven. Normally, there wouldn't even be an oven so traditional dishes that require roasting, such as Peking Duck, cannot be cooked in an ordinary Chinese kitchen (in China it is available only in specialist Peking Duck restaurants)! Ironically, Peking Duck can be more conveniently cooked in a suburban kitchen in London or Melbourne than in Beijing (Peking) itself!

THE WOK

THE WOK WAS probably first developed and used in China during the fourth to the second centuries BC. It has only recently become a popular cooking utensil in the West. As more dishes have been cooked in the wok than in any other kitchen utensil in the world, I feel that I should not fail to emphasise it as an indispensable piece of equipment in the Chinese kitchen. It became popular because it could be used over an open fire. As well as being the best utensil for stir-frying, it can also be used as a steamer (by standing a round bamboo basket steamer in a wokful of boiling water); a deep-fryer; a double boiler; for braising and stewing; and for slow-simmering.

Stir-frying is a form of Chinese cooking which has become extremely popular in the West. One of the easiest (and worst) habits to get into when stir-frying is to throw all the ingredients into the wok and stir them over a high heat. What you get if you do this is a dish of mish-mash! To avoid this, you need to keep the general principles of stir-frying at the back of your mind. As a rule, stir-frying is done in two stages. First, the principal ingredients are cut into pieces — diced into small cubes, or cut into thin slices or matchsticks — they are then cooked either over a high heat to seal the food quickly, so that it will retain most of its natural juices, or over a medium heat, to retain the tenderness of the food. After this, the principal ingredients are pushed to one side away from the high heat or removed from the wok. The supplementary ingredients and sauces are then cooked at the centre of the wok where the heat is the highest. It is only in the final stage that the lightly cooked principal ingredients are returned to the hot centre of the wok to finish cooking with the supplementary ingredients in one short blaze of heat.

Sauces in China are not meant to enhance or impose flavour on the dishes, but rather to accompany and flavour the food which is the mainstay of the meal (rice, noodles, steam buns, pancakes, etc). The function of the sauce is quite different from that in Western cuisine. The last minute addition of fresh-tasting juices during stir-frying creates a unique quality in Chinese sauces. Although these sauces are often nameless, they make a significant contribution to the flavours of Chinese cuisine.

The wok is capable of cooking as quickly as a convection or microwave oven. The microwave is not much help for instant flavour blending and generally is not of much appeal to the Chinese cook. In the long run, however, it might creep into the Chinese kitchen to be used for reheating. Many dishes are prepared for a Chinese meal, so frequently there are leftovers. Since we Chinese are traditionally thrifty, these are usually reheated for the next meal. This is where the microwave oven may one day come into its own, but by then we shall be well and truly in the twenty-first century!

THE STEAMER

ANOTHER ITEM WHICH is a prominent feature of the Chinese kitchen is the steamer; it is used much more frequently in Chinese cooking than in the West. This is probably due to the paucity of ovens and also because rice is cooked in such quantities and with such regularity that the steam generated (especially in cooking Congee or Soft Rice) should be made use of. The Chinese steamer is usually a bamboo basket attached to the top of a rice boiler. It is often made in several layers so that the dishes which require the most heat can be placed in the basket nearest the boiling water, and those which require the least heat can go in the top basket. The lid of the steamer is made of woven strips of bamboo, which enables the rising steam to pass through, rather than to condense and drip into the dishes which are being cooked.

For dishes that require a lengthy cooking time, the steamer can be used as a double boiler. If the water in the boiler is replenished with regularity, the cooking can go on indefinitely. There are a number of Chinese meat dishes, usually prepared from indifferent cuts, such as shin of beef, cow heels, pork trotters, knuckle of pork, sea-slugs and bear paws, which are cooked to a jelly-like tenderness and are considered prized delicacies! In practice, we Chinese cook only a few long-cooked dishes in the steamer. These are accompanied by one or two stir-fried dishes that have been cooked at the last moment. After all, the aim of the Chinese chef is to serve a variety of dishes which have been cooked in different ways.

In every Chinese kitchen there is usually a stockpot simmering away on the stove. Chinese stock is made by boiling chicken and duck carcasses with spare ribs. To produce a more refined stock, the Chinese add 125-250 grams (¼-½ lb) of minced chicken breast to 1.2-1.8 litres (2-3 pt) of stock to cook for 4-5 minutes before straining.

Simmering the meat in the enriched stock adds strength as well as freshness. In China this is termed Superior Broth, and is added when stock is required to flavour sauces and vegetables.

The other distinctive difference between the Western kitchen and Chinese kitchen is that the Chinese use a heavy chopping board and cleavers. The board should be a thick block from a tree trunk about 10-15 centimetres (4-6 in) thick, with the grains of the wood running vertically. It is important that the wood grains run vertically so that pieces of the board do not get chipped off easily and mixed into the food.

Chinese cleavers are extraordinarily sharp and heavy. They are used for all kinds of cutting including slicing, dicing, mincing and carving. Once you get used to using them you will never want to return to knives of a normal weight.

In the end, however, you do not require any Chinese equipment at all. You can cut with ordinary knives (as long as they are sharp), and can chop on ordinary chopping boards. You do not even need a wok. Instead you can use a deep non-stick frying pan. If you find normal domestic heat somewhat under powered, allow the oil in the pan an extra half-minute over the heat before adding the food. This initial sizzling and searing is important in maintaining flavour in stir-frying.

If you are really interested in Chinese food and cooking, your Western kitchen can easily be your Chinese kitchen. I have cooked for twenty years in a domestic Western kitchen and my only Chinese equipment is a couple of cleavers and a chopping board!

SOUP

SOUP

SOUPS PLAY A different role in a Chinese meal to the one they play in a Western meal. Chinese soups are neither starters nor additional fillers, instead they are drunk in individual spoonfuls, throughout the course of the meal. Towards the end of the meal, the last of the soup is frequently poured into the rice bowl to wash down the remaining food and grains of rice. These soups tend to be clear rather than heavy, thick soups.

This does not mean, however, that there are no thick soups in the Chinese repertoire. I suspect that many of the existing thick soups are legacies from earlier periods of Chinese culinary history. About 2000 years ago, before flour was widely used for making noodles and cakes, most Chinese cooking consisted of boiling meat, cereals, and vegetables into a thick stew. This ancient stew called keng became the accepted meal for all classes. Still prevalent today among people who require additional ballast to their meals, keng may have been the origin of the thick soup in China. In recent times, cereals and noodles have become separated from meat, fish, seafood and vegetables, and as a result dishes have become drier. To offset this drier quality, Chinese meals now include one or more savoury soups. Soups counterbalance the comparative dryness of the other food dispersed throughout the meal.

EGG-FLOWER SOUP

Dan Hua Tang

900 mL (1½ pt) strong stock
2 eggs, well beaten
1 tablespoon light soya sauce
¾ teaspoon sesame oil
1-1½ tablespoons finely chopped
  shallots (spring onions/
  scallions)
Salt, to taste
Pepper, to taste

3-4 portions

ONE OF THE MOST commonly prepared and consumed soups in China is Egg-Flower Soup, or Egg Drop Soup. It is popular because it is quick and easy to prepare.

Although the ingredients used in this soup are few and simple, the green of the spring onions and the yellow of the eggs make it quite attractive.

Method: Bring the stock to a gentle boil in a large pan. Trailing evenly, stream the beaten eggs through the prongs of a fork onto the surface of the gently simmering stock. Add the soya sauce. Stir after the eggs have set.

Serving: Pour the soup into a large serving bowl for the diners to help themselves. Sprinkle the top of the soup with sesame oil and chopped shallots. Season with salt and pepper to taste.

HOT AND SOUR SOUP

Suan La Tang

8 medium Chinese mushrooms
1.2 L (2 pt) strong beef stock
4 tablespoons wood ear fungi
2 cakes tofu (beancurd)
120-150 g (4-5 oz) cooked and
    shredded chicken meat
90 g (3 oz) shredded Sichuan Zha
    Cai pickles
1 egg, beaten
2 tablespoons green peas
1 tablespoon chopped shallots
    (spring onions/scallions)

HOT AND THICKENING SAUCE
1¼ tablespoons cornflour
    (cornstarch), blended with
    6 tablespoons water
2 tablespoons soya sauce
Ground black pepper, to taste
4-6 tablespoons wine vinegar

4-6 portions

HOT AND SOUR SOUP is a popular winter soup in China that is made from strong stock. Basic Beef Broth (page 22) is admirably suited to this purpose.

Method: Soak mushrooms in 5-6 tablespoons of boiling water for 30 minutes. Reserve the mushroom water. Remove stalks and cut caps into quarters. Add mushrooms and mushroom water to the stock. Bring to the boil and stand in the hot water for 15 minutes. Soak fungi in boiling water for 5 minutes, rinse and drain. Cut tofu into 2 cm (¾ in) cubes. Add tofu cubes, chicken, pickles, wood ear fungi, peas and shallots to the mushrooms. Bring to the boil. Pour and trail the beaten egg slowly and evenly over the surface of the soup. Stir when the egg has set.

To make the sauce, combine all the ingredients in a separate bowl until well mixed. Pour and stream it slowly into the simmering soup, which will thicken the soup and make it pronouncedly spicy.

Serving: Serve in a normal soup bowl one to each diner. In north and west China, a separate bowl of spiced mixture, containing a blend of vinegar, ground black pepper, finely chopped chillis, and sesame oil is set on the table for the diners to add to their soup in case they find the soup is not spicy enough.

CHICKEN SOUP WITH NOODLES

Ji Tang Mian

*Approximately 225-300 g
    (8-10 oz) fine Chinese egg
    noodles or vermicelli*
*180-240 g (6-8 oz) cooked chicken
    meat*
180-240 g (6-8 oz) ham
*8 tablespoons finely chopped
    shallots (spring onions/
    scallions)*
1.5 L (2½ pt) strong chicken stock
Salt, to taste
Pepper, to taste

5-6 portions

I HAVE CLASSIFIED Chicken Soup with Noodles as one of the top Chinese soups because it is an extremely popular appetizer for receptions or dinner parties. It is used, as sherry or champagne is used for receiving guests in the West, as a kind of welcoming offer — the first thing to warm the "cockles" of the visitor's heart.

It is a very simple dish which consists of boiled noodles in chicken broth. Garnish with a small amount of shredded chicken and shredded ham, and a pinch of finely chopped shallots.

Method: Cook the noodles or vermicelli by boiling them in ample water for 3-4 minutes or for the time suggested on the packet. Drain, and divide them equally between 5-6 bowls. Cut chicken and ham into matchsticks. Divide between the bowls and sprinkle evenly over the noodles. Sprinkle over the contents of each bowl a large pinch of chopped shallots.

Heat chicken stock in a saucepan. Further season with salt and pepper if necessary.

Serving: Just before serving, bring stock to the boil, then pour it evenly over the noodles and garnishing ingredients. Serve immediately.

This dish of noodles must be served hot to convey warmth of welcome.

CHICKEN AND MUSHROOM SOUP

Dong Gu Ji Tang

250 g (½ lb) chicken breast
Salt, to taste
2 tablespoons cornflour
   (cornstarch)
1 eggwhite, beaten
8 button mushrooms
8-10 medium Chinese dried
   mushrooms
750 mL (1¼ pt) strong chicken
   stock
2 slices root ginger
Pepper, to taste
1½ tablespoons light soya sauce

4-5 portions

AGAINST THE DARK brown soup, the slices of chicken coated in eggwhite and cornflour should appear resplendently white. An attractive soup both visually and flavourwise, the mushroom flavour blends easily and naturally with the neutral savouriness of the chicken.

I well remember being with my mother at the famous Hsing-Ya restaurant, Shanghai, in the 1920s. While I was blissfully sipping this soup, Noel Coward may well have been writing his *Private Lives* in the Cathay Hotel up the road.

Method: Cut chicken into 2.5 x 1.5 cm (1 x ½ in) slices. Sprinkle with salt and dredge in cornflour. Coat with eggwhite. Fry in hot oil for 1 minute and drain. Remove the stems of the button mushrooms, wash thoroughly, and cut caps into 6 thin slices. Soak dried mushrooms in 300 mL (½ pt) of boiling water for 30 minutes. Remove stem. Cut each cap into 10 thin slices. Return the sliced dried mushrooms to the mushroom water to extract more flavour.

Add the dried mushrooms and mushroom water to a large pan containing the chicken stock. Bring contents to a gentle boil. Add ginger, salt and pepper to taste. Simmer gently for 10 minutes. Add the button mushrooms, chicken and the soya sauce. Simmer gently for a further 10 minutes.

Serving: Pour the soup into individual bowls.

BASIC BEEF BROTH

Niu Rou Qing Tang

2 kg (4 lb) neck of beef or any
   stewing beef
4.2 L (7 pt) cold water
3 slices root ginger
Salt, to taste

4 portions

THIS IS SUITABLE for making various beef broth
soups, such as Beef Broth and Spinach Soup with
Tofu (beancurd).

Method: Cut beef into 2.5 cm (1 in) cubes. Place in
1.8 L (3 pt) of cold water and refrigerate for 3 hours.
Drain, then add the remaining quantity of water to
the beef. Bring contents to the boil. Reduce heat and
simmer for 2 hours, skimming every 30 minutes. Add
the ginger and salt; simmer for 35 minutes. Strain
retaining the beef cubes. The broth can now be used
in other dishes.

   The beef cubes **may be** lightly sprinkled with soya
sauce, chopped ginger and garlic, and served with
rice.

PAINTED SOUP
Hua Tang

2-3 eggwhites
Shredded Pork and Sichuan Zha
*   Cai Pickle Soup with*
*   Transparent Noodles (page 27)*

4-6 portions

WE CHINESE CAN no more paint on soup than walk on water! To prepare a surface to paint or lay a design on, you simply beat the eggwhites until stiff. Fill a soup tureen two-thirds full of soup — Shredded Pork and Sichuan Zha Cai Pickle Soup with Transparent Noodles is ideal for this purpose — then, while it is still hot, spread the eggwhite thickly over the top. The surface of the eggwhite can be smoothed over with the side of a knife blade or a spatula. Once the eggwhite surface is smooth, any kind of design can be placed on it.

Chinese chefs often create tranquil rural scenes, such as a fisherman dangling a fishing line through a hole in the eggwhite! They often use the yellow-brown Golden Needle (Tiger Lily) buds for trunks of trees; thinly sliced green vegetables for foliage and leaves; cut discs of carrots for the sun; and tomato skins as blazing red flowers. For a banquet, the more ambitious chef creates pictures of people and animals to further enliven the scene.

Serving: The soup should be warm when it is brought to the table. The host or hostess ladles part of the picture and a portion of the soup into the individual bowls of the diners. Painted Soup will add fun to any dinner party.

BEEF BROTH AND SPINACH SOUP WITH TOFU (BEANCURD)

Bo Cai Doufu Tang

375 g (12 oz) young spinach
1 cake tofu (beancurd)
1.5 L (2½ pt) Basic Beef Broth
    (page 22)
Salt, to taste
Pepper, to taste
2 slices root ginger
1½ tablespoons light soya sauce

4-5 portions

BECAUSE IT CONTAINS spinach and tofu (beancurd), this is a nourishing soup that will be quite acceptable to health-conscious Westerners.

Method: Wash spinach thoroughly and cut leaves into 5 cm (2 in) wide horizontal slices. Cut tofu into 2.5 cm (1 in) cubes. Bring beef broth to the boil in a large saucepan or casserole. Add the salt, pepper and ginger together with the spinach, tofu and soya sauce. Simmer gently for 15 minutes.

Serving: Divide the contents evenly into soup bowls and serve.

WHOLE CHICKEN SOUP WITH CHINESE CABBAGE

Bai Cai Ji Tang

1 chicken (approximately 2.25 kg/
*   5-5½ lb)*
5-6 slices root ginger
2 medium onions, sliced
Salt, to taste
Pepper, to taste
2.2 L (4 pt) strong chicken stock
1 medium Chinese white cabbage
*   (approximately 1-1.5 kg/2-3 lb)*
2 tablespoons light soya sauce
4-5 tablespoons dry sherry

8-10 portions with other dishes

THIS RICH AND LIGHT soup is a welcoming savoury part of any multi-dish Chinese meal. It is often cooked for at least 2½ hours in an earthenware pot placed inside a steamer. In the West it is best cooked as a large casserole placed in an oven preheated to 200°C (400°F/Gas mark 6) for 1¼ hours, then at 180°C (360°F/Gas mark 4) for 1½ hours.

Method: Remove the innards and the other unwanted parts of the chicken. Wash and dry the chicken inside and out and transfer the bird to a casserole. Add ginger and onion. Sprinkle the bird with salt and pepper. Add stock and heat to boiling point. Transfer to the oven preheated to 200°C (400°F/Gas mark 6). Cook for 1¼ hours. Meanwhile, trim and wash the cabbage. Cut the cabbage into 10 lengthwise strips. Insert these strips underneath the chicken while turning over the bird. Add soya sauce, and sherry. Return to the oven heated to 180°C (360°F/Gas mark 4) for a further 1¼ hours.

Serving: The dish should be served directly from the casserole. The chicken meat will be tender enough to be broken into pieces with a pair of chopsticks, and then divided into the individual bowls of the diners. The cabbage can be served in the same manner.

SOUP OF THREE DELICIOUSNESS

San Xian Tang

120-150 g (4-5 oz) chicken breast
1 eggwhite, lightly beaten
Salt, to taste
1 tablespoon cornflour (cornstarch)
1½ tablespoons dried prawns
    (shrimps)
120-150 g (4-5 oz) asparagus
120 g (4 oz) bamboo shoots
5-6 fresh scallops, removed from
    shells
5-6 king prawns (large shrimps),
    peeled with central vein
    removed
1.2 L (2 pt) strong chicken stock
2 slices root ginger
1½ tablespoons dry sherry or rice
    wine
Pepper, to taste

4-5 portions

THERE IS A LOT of poetic licence used in Chinese culinary expressions. Originally this soup contained only three delicious ingredients: fresh prawns, fresh scallops and bamboo shoots but you may also include dried shrimps and asparagus. The main concept, however, should not vary too much from the principles that the soup should be lightly cooked and the flavour should be an amalgam of light, neutral and savoury.

Method: Cut chicken into 4 x 2.5 cm (1½ x 1 in) thin slices. Wet with eggwhite, and dust with combined salt and cornflour. Poach in boiling water for 1 minute, then drain. Boil with dried prawns in 600 mL (1 pt) of water for 5 minutes and leave to simmer gently a further 5 minutes, then drain.

Cut asparagus and bamboo shoots slantwise into 1.5 cm (½ in) pieces. Cut the scallops and king prawns into halves. Poach in boiling water for 1 minute, then drain.

Heat stock in an earthenware or enamel pot. Add chicken, dried prawns, ginger, bamboo shoots, asparagus and rice wine or sherry. Bring to a gentle boil and simmer for 5 minutes. Add king prawns and scallops and continue simmering for a further 2½ minutes. Adjust for seasoning and serve.

Serving: This is an excellent light soup to serve at a party where varieties of dishes are served during the course of the meal.

SHREDDED PORK AND SICHUAN ZHA CAI PICKLE SOUP WITH TRANSPARENT NOODLES
Zha Cai Rou Si Fen Si

4 medium Chinese dried
   mushrooms
1½ tablespoons dried prawns
   (shrimps)
1.2 L (2 pt) chicken stock
90 g (3 oz) Zha Cai pickles
120 g (4 oz) bamboo shoots
120 g (4 oz) lean pork
90 g (3 oz) transparent pea starch
   noodles
Salt, to taste
Pepper, to taste

4-6 portions

THE ZHA CAI PICKLE from Sichuan has a very distinctive and spicy flavour. It is often added to other foods to inject more zest. Here, it is combined with shredded pork and transparent pea starch noodles to produce one of the most frequently served soups in China.

Method: Soak dried mushrooms and dried prawns in 300 mL (½ pt) of boiling water for 30 minutes. Retain the mushroom water. Remove and discard the stem of the mushrooms, cut caps into shreds. Add the shredded mushroom, dried shrimps and mushroom water to the chicken stock.

Rinse and wash the pickles under running water. Cut pickles, bamboo shoots and pork into matchsticks. Soak noodles in hot or boiling water for 5 minutes, drain and cut into 7.5 cm (3 in) length sections.

Heat the chicken stock and mushroom water in a large saucepan. When they start to boil add pork, pickles, and remaining ingredients. Simmer gently for 12-15 minutes. Serve.

Serving: The soup should be served in a large bowl for the diners to help themselves with a communal spoon. The soup is slightly spicy so the diner may prefer to drink a mouthful or two at a time throughout the meal rather than all at once.

RICE AND NOODLES

RICE AND NOODLES

RICE is still the principal bulk food eaten in China. Although, since the advent of the electric rice-cooker, the cooking of rice has become largely automatic and only requires going through the simplest motions. The actual preparation of cooking rice in an ordinary saucepan is still useful to be familiar with. I often receive enquiries about how to cook rice, not infrequently from Chinese who have forgotton how to do it!

Next to rice, noodles are probably the most widely eaten bulk food in China. Noodles are made from wheat flour, which is widely available in the north, as well as from rice flour, a product of the south and the Yangzi (Yangtze) River Valley.

There is some debate as to who actually invented noodles. One theory is that the Italians taught the Chinese how to make and use them via Marco Polo. I believe that this is most unlikely as the use of flour for making pasta became very widespread in China at about the time of Julius Caesar. Besides, having gone through the *Memoirs of Marco Polo* with some care in the British Museum a few years ago, I never came across any mention of noodles at all. Although, there were lengthy descriptions of Chinese markets and eating establishments, which bettered anything he had seen in Europe. Furthermore, Chinese historical records state that the first recorded millionaires in Chinese history were flour merchants who lived during the pre-Christian eras of the *Warring Kingdoms* and the early *Han Dynasty*. These merchants very probably made their money by selling cakes and noodles! It seems most likely that the Italians and the Chinese have both made their own discoveries about pasta quite independently of each other, and over the centuries each has developed its own tradition. The Italians use grated cheese and tomato for flavour and sauce, while the Chinese prepare and present their noodle dishes in the following ways:

● *Soup Noodles* (Tang Mian) — garnished noodles served in bowls in clear soups.

● *Braised or Pot-Cooked Noodles* (Hui Mian) — where noodles are pot-cooked in gravy or thickened sauce and served garnished in bowls.

● *Hot-Tossed or Cold-Tossed Noodles* (Ban Mian) — boiled noodles are served tossed together in a savoury or a nutty aromatic sauce, and are often garnished with shredded meat and vegetables.

● *Stir-fried Noodles* (Chao Mian) — the best known Chinese noodle dish in the west. Noodles are stir-fried together with meat, seafood or vegetables and are served on a plate rather than in a bowl. The stir-fried ingredients are used to garnish the noodles. When the noodles are fried until crisp and brown, the dish is called *Double Brown Noodles* (Lian Wang Mian). The stir-fried ingredients are pushed to one side of the wok, more oil is added and the noodles are shallow fried until crisp. The one drawback of this dish is that, like fried bread, it is often too greasy for contemporary taste!

BOILED RICE

Bai Fan

500 g (1 lb) long grain rice
600 mL (1 pt) water

4-6 portions

BOILED RICE for the average dinner should be fairly dry, as it is usually consumed with food which is served with ample sauce.

We Chinese are aware that there will be quite a number of savoury dishes to be consumed with the rice. So we are content that the rice served is plain and basic.

Method: Place rice in a saucepan. Rinse a couple of times and drain away the water. Add roughly 1½ cups of water to each cup of rice. Bring contents to the boil and cover with a well-fitting lid. After 3-4 minutes, reduce the heat and simmer gently for 8-9 minutes. Turn the heat off completely, and leave the rice to cook under cover in its own steam for another 8-9 minutes. The rice will then be ready to serve.

BASIC FRIED RICE

Chao Fan

1-2 medium onions, chopped
2-3 tablespoons vegetable oil
2 eggs, beaten
500 g (1 lb) boiled rice
Salt, to taste

4-6 portions

FRIED RICE IS more often served in Chinese restaurants in the West than it is in China. Many Westerners are not used to eating plain boiled rice, which they find tasteless or even insipid on its own. Basic Fried Rice is prepared by stir-frying beaten eggs and chopped onion with cooked rice (usually cold leftover rice from a previous meal). The fried onion provides the aroma, the eggs the richness, and the salt, a touch of flavour.

Method: Stir-fry the onion for about 1½ minutes in the oil, then add the eggs. Once the eggs have set, add the rice, and salt to taste. Stir until evenly mixed.

Serving: Consume with the other dishes, meat, fish, seafood, or vegetables, that are being served.

YANGZHOU FRIED RICE

Yangzhou Chao Fan

2-3 tablespoons vegetable oil
Ham, chopped
Prawns (shrimps), peeled
500 g (1 lb) boiled rice
1-2 medium onions, chopped
Peas
Carrots
2 eggs, beaten
Salt, to taste

4-6 portions

YANGZHOU IS A riverside town on the lower Yangzi (Yangtze) River. Here freshwater produce, such as prawns (shrimps), crabs and fish, and all varieties of vegetables abound. The famous ham of this region is called the Jin Hua ham. Chopped Jin Hua ham and peeled prawns (shrimps) are stir-fried with basic fried rice, and one or two vegetables, such as peas. This dish came to be called Yangzhou Fried Rice or Superior Fried Rice. In reality it is a pretty loose term, which in restaurants applies to almost any enriched fried rice where several ingredients are added, such as diced chicken or beef. When these ingredients are stir-fried with the onions, chopped ham, peas and diced carrots, the rice will be so rich that it can be eaten on its own. However, out of sheer habit, the Chinese diner will still order a couple of savoury dishes to complement the rice. This is a useful dish to cook when you have a lot of leftover ingredients to use up, as in most restaurants! It can be very tasty as well as a substantial and acceptable dish.

Method: There is no hard and fast rule for cooking Yangzhou Fried Rice. The main procedure is to stir-fry the chopped ingredients in quick sequence, and toss them all together only towards the end.

CONGEE

Zhou

*250-315 g (8-10 oz) long grain or
    short grain rice*
2.2-2.5 L (4-4½ pt) water

4-6 portions

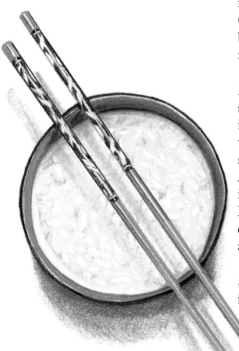

I WOULD CLASSIFY Congee or Soft Rice as one of the most memorable dishes of China. It is given to you when you are very young, very old or an invalid. One of the most digestible foods in the world, as it is warm and settling to the stomach, it is served at breakfast and supper. On both occasions, bowls of Congee are served with a selection of cold foods, such as Salt Eggs, Soya Eggs, and 100-Year-Old Eggs (1000-Year-Old Eggs), as well as a variety of pickled vegetables, Chinese wind-dried sausages and leftovers. The leftovers gain a new lease of life when eaten with this hot rice porridge, and the rice imparts a cheerfulness to these dishes which could never be revived by conventional reheating. Many Chinese look forward to their early morning breakfast as well as their midnight or "*après* mahjong" supper.

Method: Add the water and the rice to a heavy-based saucepan. Bring contents to the boil, and immediately reduce heat. Simmer very gently, without closing the lid, stirring every now and then so that no rice gets stuck to the bottom of the pan. After at least an hour and a half, test the rice to see if it is the right consistency (it should be like porridge). If it is getting too thick add a little boiling water and continue to simmer, stirring every now and then for a further 30 minutes until the rice is tender.

Serving: Congee is attractively presented in individual bowls for each diner.

SAVOURY SOFT RICE

Mei Wei Zhou

2.2 L (4 pt) chicken stock
250 g (8 oz) long grain or short
  grain rice
1½ tablespoons dried prawns
  (shrimps)
1½ tablespoons soya sauce
1 tablespoon finely chopped shallots
  (spring onions/scallions) or
  chives

4-6 portions

BASIC CONGEE CAN be transformed into Savoury Soft Rice simply by cooking the rice in chicken stock instead of water and adding dried prawns (shrimps) and soya sauce.

Method: Add the stock and the rice to a heavy-based saucepan. Bring contents to the boil, and immediately reduce the heat. Simmer gently, without completely closing the lid, and stir occasionally. Check the rice after 1½ hours. It should be the consistency of porridge, if it is too thick, add a little boiling water. Add the dried prawns and soya sauce and cook for 30 minutes.

Serving: Garnish with finely chopped shallots or chives just before serving. To the average Westerner this slight touch of savouriness will make a world of difference in the acceptability of Soft Rice.

HAINAN CHICKEN RICE

Hai Nan Ji Fan

1 chicken weighing about 2.5 kg
   (4½-5 lb)
500 g (1 lb) young leeks
2 medium onions, thinly sliced
3 slices root ginger, shredded
Salt, to taste
Pepper, to taste
500 g (1 lb) long grain rice

FOR THE SAUCE BOATS
(to dip chicken pieces in)

Soya sauce, vinegar, sesame oil,
   fresh chilli (hot pepper), root
   ginger, shallot (spring onion/
   scallion) and garlic (blend
   ingredients to taste)

6-7 portions

THIS SATISFYING DISH can be eaten on its own.

Method: Clean and remove the innards from the chicken. Chop chicken through bones into bite-size pieces. Clean leeks thoroughly and cut slantwise into 4 cm (1½ in) length sections. Place the chicken pieces and onion in a large, deep wok. Add 3 L (5 pt) of water, ginger, salt and pepper to taste. Bring contents to the boil and simmer gently for 45 minutes. Pour away three-quarters of the stock into a basin to put aside for later use for producing cups of plain chicken broth.

Rinse the rice and add it with leeks to the chicken and remaining stock in the wok. Cover and bring contents to a very gentle boil for 20 minutes. Turn off heat. Allow time for the rice to absorb all the stock and complete cooking in its own heat for a further 15 minutes under cover.

Serving: When ready to serve, heat the wok for about 1 minute, bring it to the dining table and open the lid in a great cloud of steam. The wok containing the rice and chicken should be surrounded by an array of small sauce bowls, each containing mixtures of soya sauce, vinegar, sesame oil, chopped chilli, ginger, shallot and garlic so diners can dip their pieces of chicken in to give them additional zest. Mouthfuls of rice cooked in stock should be eaten washed down with a cupful of reserved, reheated and seasoned chicken broth.

NOODLES TOSSED IN SESAME PASTE OR PEANUT BUTTER

Ma Jiang Ban Mian

500 g (1 lb) wheat flour noodles or
   spaghetti
3 tablespoons soya sauce
2 tablespoons vinegar
1½ tablespoons vegetable oil
3 shallots (spring onions/scallions)

SAUCE

2 tablespoons sesame paste or
   2 tablespoons peanut butter
1½ tablespoons vegetable oil
1 tablespoon sesame oil
1½ tablespoons stock

3 portions

I AM INCLUDING this noodle recipe because it is amazing that such a simple dish, which is prepared from inexpensive ingredients, could be so perennially appealing to such a wide number of people. I used to thoroughly enjoy tucking into a bowl of these noodles bought from a wayside stall on my way back from school in the 1920s.

Method: Place the noodles or spaghetti in a pan of boiling water, cook according to packet directions and drain. Divide the noodles between as many bowls as there are people eating.

   To make the sauce, combine ingredients in a bowl until well blended.

Serving: Allow each diner to sprinkle an equal amount of soya sauce, vinegar, oil and finely chopped shallots over their own bowl of noodles. Top with sauce. The appeal of the dish lies in its being nutty, savoury and aromatic. The freshly chopped shallots, sesame oil and paste on hot noodles releases an appetizing aroma.

PEKING JA JIANG MIAN

Beijing Zha Jiang Mian

500 g (1 lb) wheat flour noodles or spaghetti
1 medium cucumber, cut into matchsticks

SAUCE

4 tablespoons vegetable oil
250 g (½ lb) minced pork
1 medium onion, finely chopped
2 slices root ginger, finely chopped
2 cloves garlic, finely chopped
2 tablespoons yellow bean sauce
2 tablespoons dark soya sauce
2 tablespoons tomato purée
3 tablespoons stock
1 tablespoon cornflour (cornstarch) blended with 4 tablespoons water

4 portions

THIS DISH HAS a curious resemblance to the Italian "Spaghetti Bolognaise", but it has shredded cucumber tossed in with the noodles and meat sauce, adding a crunchy texture to the dish. The use of soya sauce makes it more savoury than using only tomato sauce, as in the Italian version.

Method: Place the noodles or spaghetti in a pan of boiling water and cook for the length of time specified on the packet. Drain.

To make the sauce, heat the oil in a wok or deep frying pan. When hot, add the minced pork, onion, ginger and garlic. Mix and turn over medium heat for 3 minutes. Pour in 100 mL (⅙ pt) boiling water. Raise heat to high. Bring contents to the boil. Add yellow bean sauce, soya sauce, tomato purée and stock. Stir while the sauce boils and reduces by half. Stir in the blended cornflour, which should thicken the sauce.

Serving: Place noodles in the middle of a large, well-heated serving plate, and surround them with a thick bank of shredded cucumber. Pour the meat sauce on top of the noodles. Bring the dish to the dining table for the diners to toss the meat sauce and noodles together, while still hot.

SHANGHAI COLD-TOSSED NOODLES

Shang Hai Leng Mian

*2 tablespoons Chinese dried
   prawns (shrimps)*
2 tablespoons dry sherry
2 tablespoons wine vinegar
2 teaspoons chilli sauce
3 tablespoons soya sauce
*500 g (1 lb) fresh wheat flour
   noodles or spaghetti*
*2½ tablespoons Sichuan hot Zha
   Cai pickles, chopped*
*2 tablespoons Chinese green
   mustard Snow Pickles, chopped*
*2 tablespoons Chinese Dong Cai
   Winter Pickles, chopped*
*3 shallots (spring onions/scallions),
   cut diagonally into 1.5 cm
   (½ in) lengths*
1 teaspoon sesame oil

4-5 portions

DURING THE HOT summer in Shanghai this is one of
the favourite dishes eaten.

Method: Soak the dried prawns in hot water for 10
minutes. Drain and chop them coarsely. Add sherry
to the chopped prawns to marinate briefly. Combine
the vinegar, chilli sauce and soya sauce, and mix
them well.

   If using freshly made noodles, simmer them in a
pan of boiling water for approximately 2 minutes.
Drain and cool. If using ordinary Chinese wheat flour
noodles, boil them for approximately 6 minutes, drain
and cool. If using spaghetti, follow packet directions,
drain and cool.

Serving: Spread the noodles on a large serving plate.
Sprinkle them evenly with coarsely chopped pickles,
chopped prawns and sherry, and then the soya sauce
mixture. Add the shallots and sesame oil.

   To serve in the Chinese way, place the large
serving plate at the centre of the table. Allow the
diners themselves to toss and mix the noodles with
different ingredients, according to individual
preference.

BASIC SHREDDED PORK CHAO MIAN

Rou Si Chao Mian

*250-315 g (8-10 oz) wheat flour
noodles or spaghetti*
180 g (6 oz) pork belly
Salt, to taste
Pepper, to taste
3 shallots (spring onions/scallions)
*60 g (2 oz) Sichuan hot Zha Cai
pickles*
3 tablespoons vegetable oil
2 slices root ginger, crushed
2 cloves garlic, crushed
120 g (4 oz) beansprouts
2 tablespoons soya sauce
*1½ tablespoons prawn (shrimp)
sauce*
6 tablespoons stock

2-3 portions

NOODLES ARE CONSUMED as snacks in China. During a meal, they are eaten with rice and are regarded as adding weight and substance.

Method: Boil the noodles for approximately 6 minutes (follow packet directions for spaghetti) and drain. Rinse under running water to separate. Cut pork, across lean and fat, into 1 cm (⅓ in) matchsticks. Sprinkle and rub with salt and pepper. Cut shallots into 1.5 cm (½ in) sections and separate the green parts from the white. Shred the pickles.

Heat 2 tablespoons of oil in a wok or large frying pan. When hot add the pork, ginger and garlic, the whites of the shallots and the shredded pickles. Stir-fry them together over high heat for 2½ minutes. Remove half the contents and put them aside. Add half the soya sauce, half the prawn sauce and half the stock. Bring contents to the boil. Add the noodles. Stir-fry and turn over medium heat for 2 minutes. Remove and transfer the contents onto a large serving dish.

Heat the remaining tablespoon of oil. When hot, return the portion set aside earlier to the wok/pan. Stir-fry over high heat for 1½ minutes, adding beansprouts, the remaining soya sauce, prawn sauce and stock, and the greens of the shallots. Stir and turn them all together for ¾ minute over high heat.

Serving: Remove all the ingredients from the wok and place them as garnish on top of the noodles piled up on the serving plate. Serve with extra shredded pickles.

BRAISED BIRTHDAY NOODLES WITH RED-COOKED PORK

Hong Shao Zhu Rou Shou Mian

500 g (1 lb) lean pork belly
2 cloves garlic, chopped
2 slices root ginger, chopped
2 teaspoons sugar
3 tablespoons rice wine
5 tablespoons dark soya sauce
300 mL (½ pt) water
300 mL (½ pt) strong stock
1 tablespoon cornflour (cornstarch)
   blended with 4 tablespoons
   water
180 g (6 oz) French beans (string
   beans)
250 g (8 oz) Chinese wheat flour
   noodles or egg noodles
2 soya eggs or hard-boiled eggs

4 portions

IN CHINA, THE EGG symbolises continuity and fertility so it is frequently included in birthday dishes. In this recipe, the top of each bowl of noodles is decorated with half a hard-boiled egg or soya egg (an egg which has been hard-boiled in soya sauce).

Method: To prepare the red-cooked pork, cut the pork through the skin, including the lean-and-fat, into 5 x 2.5 cm (2 x 1 in) pieces. Stir-fry the pork pieces in a pan with garlic, ginger, sugar and rice wine for 3 minutes. Add the soya sauce and water, and simmer over very low heat for 1 hour.
Add stock and simmer for a further 15 minutes.
Stir in the blended cornflour to thicken the sauce.
   Wash and cut off the ends of the beans. Place the noodles with the beans in a heavy pot or casserole and cook for 5 minutes. Pour the pork and gravy over the noodles and beans. Simmer gently together until the noodles are cooked and have absorbed the flavour of the pork sauce.

Serving: Divide the noodles and sauce into four large bowls. Decorate by topping each with half a soya egg or hard-boiled egg.

LAMB AND LEEK MANCHURIAN BRAISED NOODLES

Man Zhou Da Suan Yang Rou Mian

875 g (1¾ lb) leg of lamb
Salt, to taste
Pepper, to taste
Cornflour (cornstarch) for
　dredging
375 g (¾ lb) young leeks
4 tablespoons vegetable oil
3 slices root ginger, shredded
3 cloves garlic, crushed
900 mL (1½ pt) strong stock
3 tablespoons light soya sauce
4 tablespoons rice wine or dry
　sherry
375 g (12 oz) Chinese wheat flour
　noodles or spaghetti
1 tablespoon sesame oil

4-5 portions

CONSUMING THIS SOUP is a very warming experience!

Method: Cut the lamb into bite-size 4 cm (1½ in) cubes. Rub with salt and pepper, and dredge in cornflour. Clean leeks thoroughly, and cut slantwise into 5 cm (2 in) sections.

Heat oil in a heavy saucepan. When hot, add ginger, garlic and lamb. Stir-fry, turning for 5 minutes. Add 600 mL (1 pt) stock and bring to the boil. Reduce heat to low and simmer gently for 1 hour.

Add the leeks and the remaining stock to the stew. Bring to the boil again. Simmer gently together for 5 minutes. Add the soya sauce and wine. Add noodles or spaghetti and cook according to packet directions. Sprinkle lightly with sesame oil and serve.

Serving: Divide the noodles, lamb and leeks among the diners' bowls and serve every one with chopsticks (rather than spoons), as they are expected to drink the ample soup by lifting the bowls to their mouths.

TEN TREASURE BRAISED TRANSPARENT PEA STARCH NOODLES

Shi Jin Fen Si

4 medium Chinese dried
   mushrooms
90 g (3 oz) pork
90 g (3 oz) chicken breasts
120 g (4 oz) celery
60 g (2 oz) bamboo shoots
2 shallots (spring onions/scallions)
90 g (3 oz) French beans (string
   beans)
1 small red capsicum (sweet
   pepper)
185 g (6 oz) pea starch noodles or
   spaghetti
1½ tablespoons Chinese dried
   prawns (shrimps)
5 tablespoons vegetable oil
2 slices bacon, cut into matchsticks
1 medium onion, thinly sliced
2 slices root ginger, chopped
2 cloves garlic, chopped
300 mL (½ pt) strong stock
2 tablespoons soya sauce
3 tablespoons dry sherry
Dash sesame oil

6-10 portions

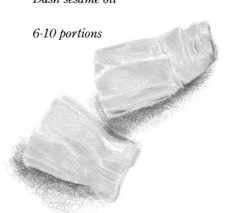

THIS IS ONE of the favourite dishes in the Liberation Army. Simply called the Big Pot Dish (Da Huo Cai), it makes a spartan army meal of plain rice more palatable!

Method: Soak dried mushrooms in 150 mL (¼ pt) boiling water for 30 minutes. Reserve mushroom water and cut caps into shreds, discarding stems. Cut pork, chicken, celery, bamboo shoots, shallots, French beans and red capsicum into matchsticks. Immerse noodles in hot water for 15 minutes or if using spaghetti, boil for 5 minutes, cut into 10 cm (4 in) sections and drain thoroughly. Soak dried prawns in hot water for 15 minutes. Drain and chop finely.

Heat 3 tablespoons of oil in a saucepan. When hot, add the prawns, dried mushrooms, bacon and onion. Stir-fry them together over medium heat for 5 minutes. Pour in the mushroom water. Bring contents to the boil. Add the pea starch noodles or spaghetti and stir them through. Set aside.

Heat remaining oil in a saucepan. When hot, add ginger, garlic, celery, bamboo shoots, shallots, shredded pork and chicken, and stir-fry them together over medium heat for 4-5 minutes. Add French beans, capsicum, stock, and pour in the soya sauce and sherry. Cook gently together for 5 minutes.

In the final phase add the contents of the first pan to the second pan. Mix together and heat through for 5 minutes or until noodles are cooked.

Serving: Lace with a dash of sesame oil and serve.

CANTONESE HE FEN NOODLES WITH BEEF IN BLACK BEAN SAUCE

Chi Zhi Niu He

375 g (12 oz) He Fen noodles
3 shallots (spring onions/scallions)
500 g (1 lb) lean beef, such as
    rump, fillet or topside
Salt, to taste
1 eggwhite, lightly beaten
1½ tablespoons cornflour
    (cornstarch)
4 tablespoons vegetable oil
2 medium onions, thinly sliced
2 slices root ginger, shredded
2 cloves garlic, crushed
1 medium red capsicum (sweet
    pepper), cut in strips

SAUCE

2 tablespoons salted black beans,
    soaked in hot water for
    3 minutes, then chopped
1¼ tablespoons cornflour
    (cornstarch) blended with
    4 tablespoons water
2 tablespoons soya sauce
1½ tablespoons oyster sauce
1 tablespoon chilli sauce
4 tablespoons stock

4-5 portions

HE FEN NOODLES ARE flat ribbon rice flour noodles which are generally sold freshly made. The attraction of this dish lies principally in its beefy flavour and the spicy and earthy black beans.

Method: Place noodles in a saucepan of boiling water to simmer for 5 minutes. Drain and rinse under running water to separate. Cut shallots diagonally into 5 cm (2 in) sections. Cut beef into 4 x 1.5 cm (1½ x ½ in) strips. Rub with salt, wet with eggwhite and dredge in cornflour.

Heat oil in a wok or large frying pan. When hot add the onions, ginger and garlic; stir-fry for 1½ minutes and push them to one side of the pan. Add beef and black beans to the centre of the wok. Thicken the sauce by stirring in the blended cornflour. Bring the onions, ginger and garlic back to the mix and stir with the other sauce ingredients. Cook together for 1 minute. Remove half the beef and sauce from the wok, cover and set aside. Add the noodles to the remaining beef and sauce mixture. Stir together over medium heat for 1½ minutes.

Serving: Transfer the contents of the wok or pan onto a large serving plate. Add the shallots and shredded capsicum to the wok together with the beef and sauce which has been put aside. Stir-fry for 30 seconds over high heat. Pour over beef on the serving plate to garnish.

SINGAPORE RICE-STICK NOODLES

Xing Zhou Chao Mi

375 g (12 oz) packet of rice flour
    noodles
3 tablespoons Chinese dried
    prawns (shrimps)
180 g (6 oz) Cantonese Cha Shao
    roast pork
2 shallots (spring onions/scallions),
    cut diagonally
3 tablespoons vegetable oil
2 small onions, thinly sliced
2 slices bacon, cut into matchsticks
Salt, to taste
2½ tablespoons curry powder or to
    taste
5 tablespoons stock
90 g (3 oz) cooked prawns
    (shrimps)
1½ tablespoons light soya sauce
180 g (6 oz) beansprouts

4-5 portions

THIS IS NOT EXACTLY the most refined of Chinese dishes, but it is very popular and often appears on the menus of Chinese restaurants abroad. The mild curry flavour gives the dish its South Sea character and zest. It is an excellent filler.

Method: Soak noodles in warm water for 5 minutes and drain thoroughly. Soak dried prawns in a small bowl of boiling water for 15 minutes and chop roughly. Cut Cha Shao roast pork into 5 x 2.5 cm (2 x 1 in) thin slices and shallots into 4 cm (1½ in) sections.

Heat 2 tablespoons of oil in a wok or frying-pan. When hot, add onions, dried, soaked prawns and bacon, and stir-fry over medium heat for 1½ minutes. Add salt and 2 tablespoons curry powder, and stir-fry for a further minute. Add stock and stir to form a bubbling sauce. Add the noodles and stir to coat with the sauce.

Heat remaining oil in a separate wok or pan. When hot, add the cooked prawns, sliced roast pork, soya sauce and the additional ½ tablespoon of curry powder. Stir-fry for about a minute. Add the beansprouts and shallots, turn the heat up high and stir-fry all the ingredients together for just over a minute.

Serving: Combine the contents of the two woks, toss and turn a few times and serve on one large serving plate.

HOT-TOSSED NOODLES WITH ASPARAGUS
Lu Sun Ban Mian

*250-315 g (8-10 oz) Chinese wheat
   flour noodles or spaghetti
185 g (6 oz) asparagus
150 mL (¼ pt) strong stock
2 tablespoons vegetable oil
2 cloves garlic, chopped
2 teaspoons butter
1½ tablespoons light soya sauce*

4-5 portions

SURPRISINGLY, THE COMBINATION of fresh crunchy asparagus and soft noodles in this dish appeals to people who are normally big meat-eaters!

Method: Boil the noodles or spaghetti for the time specified on the packet and drain. Remove 2.5 cm (1 in) of the tough end of the asparagus and cut diagonally into 5 cm (2 in) sections. Parboil them for 5-6 minutes and drain. Heat stock in a small saucepan. Add the asparagus to simmer in the stock for 5 minutes. Turn asparagus several times so it will cook evenly. Heat the oil in a wok or pan and add the garlic. Stir-fry over medium heat for about 1 minute, then add the asparagus, stock and the noodles and mix them for a couple of minutes.

Serving: Transfer the noodles and asparagus to a large serving plate. While still hot, dot with butter, sprinkle with soya sauce and serve. Allow the diners themselves to do the final tossing together of the noodles and asparagus on their own plates.

THREE MUSHROOM NOODLES

San Dong Mian

*10 medium or large dried
  mushrooms*
*10 medium or large fresh
  mushrooms*
*180 g (6 oz) canned Chinese straw
  mushrooms*
*250 g (8 oz) Chinese noodles or
  spaghetti*
3 tablespoons vegetable oil
*2 shallots (spring onions/scallions),
  finely chopped*
2 cloves garlic, crushed
*120-180 g (4-6 oz) Chinese canned
  braised bamboo shoots, cut into
  matchsticks*
2 tablespoons soya sauce

3-4 portions

THIS DISH IS POPULAR with mushroom lovers.

Method: Soak the dried mushrooms in a bowl of
boiling water for 1 hour. Remove and discard the
tough stems and cut caps into quarters. Reserve half
the water. Clean and cut the caps of fresh
mushrooms into quarters, also discarding the stems.
Drain the straw mushrooms, retaining half the water
from the can and add the water used for soaking the
dried mushrooms. Heat them together in a saucepan
to reduce it to half its original volume.

Boil the noodles in boiling water for 6-7 minutes.
Drain completely, and add them to simmer and soak
in the reduced mushroom water to absorb the
mushroom flavour.

Heat 2 tablespoons of oil in a frying pan. When hot
add half the shallots and garlic, and stir-fry them
with the quartered dried mushrooms for 2 minutes.
Add half the fresh mushrooms, bamboo shoots,
1 tablespoon soya sauce and the straw mushrooms
and the retained mushroom water; stir-fry them all
together for a further 3 minutes.

Add the noodles to turn with other ingredients in
the pan. Allow them to cook gently together for 3-
4 minutes or until cooked. Transfer the contents of
the pan onto a large serving plate.

Heat remaining oil in a wok or frying pan. When
hot, add the remaining garlic, shallots, bamboo
shoots, soya sauce and mushrooms. Stir-fry them
over high heat for 2½ minutes.

Serving: Lay the mushrooms and bamboo shoots as a
garnish on top of the noodles on the serving plate.

DOUBLE CRISP NOODLES WITH BEEF AND SEAFOOD

Hai Xian Niu Rou Chao Mian

*250 g (8 oz) Chinese wheat flour
    noodles or spaghetti*
150 mL (¼ pt) vegetable oil

TOPPING AND SAUCE

*180 g (6 oz) beef, such as fillet,
    rump, topside*
*120 g (4 oz) shelled prawns
    (shrimps)*
Salt, to taste
1 eggwhite, lightly beaten
*1½ tablespoons cornflour
    (cornstarch)*
*2 shallots (spring onions/scallions),
    finely chopped*
2 slices root ginger, shredded
2 cloves garlic, finely chopped
2½ tablespoons soya sauce
1½ tablespoons oyster sauce
4 tablespoons stock
*1 tablespoon cornflour (cornstarch)
    blended with 4 tablespoons
    water*

4 portions

SOME PEOPLE IN CHINA enjoy noodles which are partially crispy. Diners will find the noodles in this dish crispy on the outside but still soft on the inside. When this is allied to the topping it adds a new dimension to the whole dish.

Method: Add the noodles or spaghetti to a pan of boiling water to cook according to directions on the packet. Drain thoroughly and heat oil in a frying pan. When hot (a crumb will sizzle when dropped into it) add the noodles in a whole pad. Press them down to fry over high heat for 3-3½ minutes on either side, until both sides are slightly brown and crispy. Leaving a small amount of oil for stir-frying the toppings, drain the noodles and transfer them to a serving plate.

Prepare the beef by cutting it into 5 x 2.5 cm (2 x 1 in) thin slices. Rub the beef and the prawns with salt, wet with eggwhite, and dredge with cornflour.

Heat the remaining oil in the wok or frying pan. When hot, add the beef, prawns, shallots, ginger and garlic. Stir-fry them over high heat for 2 minutes. Add the soya sauce, oyster sauce and stock. Stir-fry, turning over high heat for 1 minute. Add blended cornflour evenly over the pan to thicken the bubbling sauce and stir in well.

Serving: Pour the sauce in the wok or pan over the noodles on the serving plate.

VEGETABLES, TOFU (BEANCURD) AND EGGS

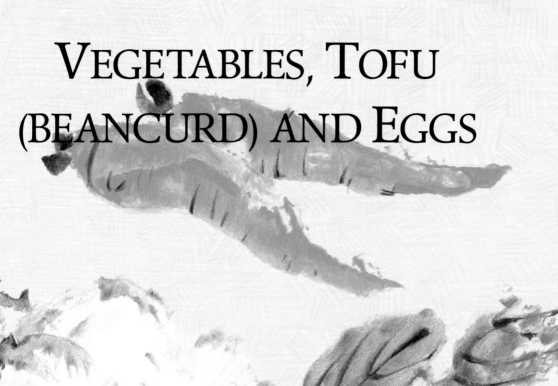

VEGETABLES,
TOFU (BEANCURD) AND EGGS

THE CHINESE EAT A large amount of vegetable-based dishes as well as huge quantities of carbohydrates, particularly rice and noodles.

Three of the most popular Chinese vegetable dishes: Kai Yang Bai Cai, Chao Bo Cai and Hong Shao Bai Cai are included here.

While many of the dishes included in this book feature meat, most Chinese do not eat many meat or dairy products, so to obtain protein they eat tofu (beancurd) and eggs.

Reputed to be richer in protein than most meat, tofu is cheaper and more easily digested. It is becoming increasingly more acceptable and popular in the health-conscious West.

Tofu is derived from soya bean purée, which has been boiled in water and then clarified and filtered for its milk. The milk is set overnight by cooking. When set, tofu has the texture of a firm custard. It is normally sold as cakes 7.5 x 7.5 cm (3 x 3 in) and about 2.5 cm (1 in) thick, which can be cut into any shape or size.

Tofu's neutral taste and opaque cream colour makes it ideal for Chinese cooking as it readily absorbs the flavours of the food it is cooked with. Because it is so versatile, it is a great boon to vegetarians.

Egg dishes are extremely popular because there is an abundance of poultry in China, they are easily prepared and are versatile. They are usually stir-fried dishes, such as omelettes (with one, two, or more ingredients added), but they also may be steamed, as in savoury custards (which are excellent to eat with plain boiled rice). The majority of Chinese egg dishes are comparatively basic and they are a mainstay of the Chinese diet.

The Chinese inclination toward compound cooking (cutting or chopping food into small pieces to be combined at different stages of cooking), means that beaten eggs are ideal to mix with meat, seafood and vegetables. This produces highly palatable dishes, which can be prepared in a minimal length of time.

STIR-FRIED CHINESE WHITE CABBAGE

Kai Yang Bai Cai

*1 medium Chinese white cabbage
    (about 500 g/1 lb)*
*2-2½ tablespoons Chinese dried
    prawns (shrimps)*
3 tablespoons vegetable oil
2 slices root ginger, shredded
Salt, to taste
1½ tablespoons light soya sauce

5-6 portions with other dishes

THIS IS ONE of the most common vegetable dishes
seen on a Chinese dining table.

Method: Clean and cut cabbage into 5 cm (2 in) slices.
Soak prawns in boiling water for 10 minutes and
drain.
   Heat oil in a saucepan. When hot, add ginger and
dried prawns and stir over medium heat for
1½ minutes. Add the cabbage, sprinkle with salt,
turn and stir for 1½ minutes. Add the soya sauce and
stir-fry for another 1½ minutes.

Serving: The dish should be served in conjunction
with other savoury dishes.

STIR-FRIED SPINACH

Chao Bo Cai

500 g (1 lb) fresh spinach
3 tablespoons vegetable oil
4-5 cloves garlic, crushed
Salt, to taste
2 shallots (spring onions/scallions),
   diced
1½ teaspoons fermented tofu
   (beancurd) cheese or Tou Si
   (optional)
1 tablespoon soya sauce

4-5 portions with other dishes

THIS IS EXCELLENT to serve with all meat and poultry dishes.

Method: Trim the spinach and wash well. Cut into 5-8 cm (2-3 in) slices.

Heat oil in a large frying pan or wok. Add garlic, salt and shallots. Stir them in the hot oil for 30 seconds. Add the tofu. Mash in the oil over medium heat. Add the spinach. Mix everything together well. Sprinkle evenly with soya sauce and cook gently for 1½ minutes. Turn and stir once more.

Serving: Serve on a well-heated plate.

RED-COOKED CHINESE CABBAGE

Hong Shao Bai Cai

1 medium Chinese cabbage,
  weighing about 700 g (1½ lb)
1½ tablespoons Chinese dried
  prawns (shrimps)
2 tablespoons vegetable oil
2 slices root ginger, shredded
2 cloves garlic, crushed
Salt, to taste
400 mL (⅔ pt) strong stock
4½ tablespoons light soya sauce
2 teaspoons sugar

5-6 portions with other dishes

CONSUME THIS DISH with quantities of plain boiled rice.

Method: Clean and cut cabbage into 5 x 8 cm (2 x 3 in) slices. Soak dried prawns in boiling water for 5 minutes and drain.

Heat oil in large saucepan. When hot add the ginger and garlic. Stir them over medium heat for 30 seconds. Add the cabbage, prawns and salt, mixing in well. Pour in the stock and bring contents to the boil. Reduce heat to low, add soya sauce and sugar. Cover and cook gently for 10-12 minutes, stirring occasionally. There is something very sumptuous about this dish.

Serving: This dish is full of gravy so it should be served in a large bowl rather than a flat serving plate.

RED-COOKED EGGPLANT (AUBERGINE)

Hong Shao Qie Zi

2 medium eggplants (aubergines)
1½ tablespoons Chinese dried
prawns (shrimps)
3 tablespoons vegetable oil
Salt, to taste
2 slices root ginger, shredded
3 cloves garlic, crushed
1 green chilli (hot pepper), seeded
and chopped
1 red dried chilli (hot pepper),
seeded and chopped
3 tablespoons light soya sauce
3 tablespoons stock
2 tablespoons rice wine or dry
sherry

5-6 portions with other dishes

THIS IS A very rich vegetable dish.

Method: Peel the eggplants and cut into the average size of chips (approximately 1.5 x 5 cm [½ x 2 in] in size). Soak dried prawns in boiling water for 10 minutes, drain and chop coarsely.

Heat oil in a wok or frying pan. When hot, add the chopped dried prawns, salt, ginger, garlic, and the chillies. Stir over medium heat for about a minute. Add the soya sauce and stock. Stir until the sauce bubbles. Add all the eggplant and stir to coat with sauce. Reduce heat to low and cook slowly for 4-5 minutes. Add the wine or sherry and stir. Leave to cook 3 more minutes and serve.

STIR-FRIED ASPARAGUS WITH GARLIC
Suan Zi Lu Sun

500 g (1 lb) young asparagus
3½ tablespoons vegetable oil
2 cloves garlic, crushed
Salt, to taste
1½ teaspoons sugar
1 tablespoon light soya sauce
3 tablespoons meat or vegetable
   stock
1 tablespoon Hai Xian (Hoisin)
   sauce
1 tablespoon prawn (shrimp) sauce
1 tablespoon cornflour (cornstarch)
   blended with 3 tablespoons
   water

4-5 portions with other dishes

THE RICH SAUCE and the asparagus combine to make this a very tasty dish. You may find the salt content in this dish to be not to your taste. If so, reduce the quantities of soya sauce, Hai Xian (Hoisin) sauce and prawn (shrimp) sauce and increase the amount of water blended with the cornflour (cornstarch).

Method: Remove and discard the tough ends of the asparagus. Cut each spear diagonally into approximately 5 cm (2 in) sections.

Heat oil in a wok or frying pan. When hot add garlic, salt and asparagus. Stir over medium heat for 2 minutes. Add the sugar, soya sauce, stock, prawn sauce and Hai Xian sauce. Stir contents over medium heat for a further ¾ minute. Reduce heat and continue to reduce the sauce for a further 1½ minutes. Add the blended cornflour and stir the contents in the wok a few more times.

SUMMER SQUASH STEW WITH TOMATOES, PEAS AND POTATOES

Shi Jin Dong Gua Tang

1.25 kg (2½ lbs) summer squash
   (dong gua)
500 g (1 lb) potatoes
4 medium tomatoes
1¼ tablespoons Chinese dried
   prawns (shrimps)
3 tablespoons vegetable oil
1 medium onion, thinly sliced
2 slices bacon, cut into matchsticks
2 slices root ginger, shredded
2 cloves garlic, crushed
600 mL (1 pt) strong meat stock
2 teaspoons sugar
3 tablespoons light soya sauce
Salt, to taste
Pepper, to taste
250 g (½ lb) peas

10 portions with other dishes

THIS IS A SEMI-SOUP dish suitable for 10 diners when served with other dishes.

Method: Carefully remove the flesh from the skin of the squash, retaining the shell for use as a serving bowl. Dice squash flesh into 2 cm (¾ in) cubes. Peel and dice potatoes into similar cubes. Skin the tomatoes and cut into quarters. Soak dried prawns in hot water for 10 minutes, drain and chop coarsely.

   Heat oil in a large saucepan. When hot, add onion, bacon, ginger, garlic, and dried prawns. Stir-fry them over medium heat for a couple of minutes. Add the diced squash and potato cubes, and stir over medium heat for 5 minutes. Pour in the stock, sugar, soya sauce, and season with salt and pepper to taste. Add the peas and the tomatoes. Bring contents to the boil and simmer gently for 20 minutes.

Serving: One of the favourite ways of serving this dish is to make use of the hollow squash shell, by placing it in a large heatproof bowl. Pour the stew from the saucepan into the squash. Place the squash shell in a steamer and steam for 5-6 minutes. The dish should be ready to serve. Bring it all steaming and piping hot to the dining table for the diners to help themselves.

MIXED SPRING VEGETABLE STEW WITH TRANSPARENT NOODLES

Ji Cai Fen Si

1½ tablespoons Chinese dried
   prawns (shrimps)
3 young carrots
1 medium cucumber
2 shallots (spring onions/scallions)
250 g (8 oz) spinach
1 lettuce
120 g (4 oz) pea starch transparent
   noodles or spaghetti
4 tablespoons vegetable oil
2 slices bacon, cut into matchsticks
2 medium onions, thinly sliced
2 slices root ginger, shredded
2 cloves garlic, chopped
250 g (8 oz) French beans (string
   beans), ends cut off and halved
250 g (8 oz) broccoli, in florets
600 mL (1 pt) strong stock
250 g (8 oz) beansprouts
4-5 medium tomatoes, quartered
2 tablespoons soya sauce
1½ tablespoons prawn (shrimp)
   sauce
2 teaspoons sesame oil

7-8 portions with other dishes

IN THE CONTEXT of a Chinese meal, this dish should be treated like a hot salad and consumed in conjunction with both meat and rice.

Method: Soak dried prawns in hot water for 10 minutes, drain and chop coarsely. Cut carrots and cucumber diagonally into 5 cm (2 in) sections, shallots into 1.5 cm (½ in) sections, spinach and lettuce into 5 cm (2 in) slices; soak transparent noodles in hot water for 5 minutes. If using spaghetti, boil for 5 minutes, then cut into 8-10 cm (3-4 in) sections.

Heat vegetable oil in a large saucepan. When hot, add dried prawns, bacon, onions, ginger, garlic and carrots, and stir-fry for 2 minutes. Add beans, broccoli, cucumber and continue to stir-fry over medium heat for a further 2 minutes. Pour in the stock and add the beansprouts, spinach, tomatoes and lettuce. Bring contents to a gentle boil, add soya sauce and prawn sauce, simmer gently for 15 minutes. Add the noodles or spaghetti, stirring to coat with sauce. Add shallots and sesame oil, and simmer stew gently for a further 6-7 minutes or until noodles or spaghetti is ready. Serve.

Serving: Because this is really a semi-soup, serve in a large bowl.

STIR-FRIED BEANSPROUTS WITH SICHUAN ZHA CAI PICKLES AND SHREDDED PORK

Zha Cai Dou Ya Rou Si

500 g (1 lb) beansprouts
2 shallots (spring onions/scallions)
3 tablespoons vegetable oil
120 g (4 oz) pork belly, cut into
    matchsticks
60 g (2 oz) Sichuan Zha Cai
    pickles, cut into matchsticks
1½ tablespoons dark soya sauce
1 tablespoon vinegar
1½ teaspoons sesame oil
Salt, to taste
Pepper, to taste

4-5 portions with other dishes

IT IS USUAL in Chinese vegetable cooking, especially when stir-frying, to incorporate meat or seafood to enhance the flavour of the dish.

Method: Wash and dry the beansprouts. Cut shallots diagonally into 2.5 cm (1 in) sections.

Heat vegetable oil in a frying pan. When hot, add pork and pickles and stir-fry over high heat for 1½ minutes. Add shallots and stir-fry for a further 30 seconds. Add the beansprouts and stir-fry for 1½ minutes. Sprinkle mixture with soya sauce, vinegar and sesame oil. Stir-fry over high heat for a further 1 minute. Season to taste with salt and pepper.

Serving: Serve hot on a well-heated plate. This dish should be accompanied by boiled rice and other savoury dishes.

BUDDHISTS' DELIGHT OR FOOD FOR THE MINOR GODS

Luo Han Zhai

DRIED INGREDIENTS

6 medium dried mushrooms
4 tablespoons wood ear fungi
4 tablespoons dried hair seaweed
4 tablespoons dried bamboo shoots
3 lily bud stems
7 g (½ oz) dried chestnuts
2 dried tofu (beancurd) sticks
120-150 g (4-5 oz) bean starch
  noodles
3½ tablespoons vegetable oil
4 tablespoons lotus nuts
4 slices dried gingko nuts
Salt, to taste
Pepper, to taste

FRESH INGREDIENTS

2 sticks celery cut into 5 cm (2 in)
  sections and shredded
75 g (2½ oz) button mushrooms
2 shallots (spring onions/scallions),
  cut into 5 cm (2 in) sections
4 large Chinese cabbage leaves
60 g (2 oz) cauliflower, in florets
75 g (2½ oz) broccoli, in florets
1 green capsicum (sweet pepper),
  cut into 1.5 cm (½ in) strips
Salt, to taste
3 tablespoons vegetable oil
2 teaspoons sesame oil

THE LUO HANS ARE minor gods whose images line the side walls of the monasteries and temples in China by the hundreds. This dish was created to feed them. It is prepared by stewing dried vegetables, fresh vegetables and bean starch transparent noodles cooked in a seasoned vegetable stock.

To serve, a very large bowl was placed at the centre of the monastery table for the monks, and presumably also the Luo Hans, to gather around and consume with massed chopsticks.

Method: Soak the dried mushrooms in hot water for 30 minutes, then drain. Remove and discard stems and cut caps into quarters. Rinse and clean wood ear fungi in warm water. Rinse and soak hair seaweed for 5 minutes and drain. Rinse dried bamboo shoots, soak for 15 minutes and cut into 5 cm (2 in) sections. Soak lily bud stems for 5 minutes in water and cut into 5 cm (2 in) sections. Soak dried chestnuts in hot water for 1 hour and cut into halves. Break tofu sticks into 5 cm (2 in) sections, soak in hot water for 25 minutes and drain. Soak noodles according to directions on the packet, drain and cut into 8 cm (3 in) sections.

Cook all the dried ingredients, except for the bean starch noodles, and the fresh ingredients separately by stir-frying them in hot oil in two woks or saucepans. Stir-fry them for 3-4 minutes each over medium heat. Finally combine the two lots of cooked foods into one large wok or pan.

SAUCE

600 mL (1 pt) strong vegetable
  stock
3 tablespoons light soya sauce
1½ tablespoons fermented tofu
  (beancurd)
3 tablespoons rice wine or dry
  sherry

6-8 portions

To make the sauce, add the stock, soya sauce, tofu, and rice wine or sherry. Bring contents to a gentle boil. Add the noodles. Stir and turn to mix evenly with other ingredients in the wok or pan. Continue to stir and simmer until the noodles are cooked. Stir and turn the ingredients over, and cook gently for the next 6-7 minutes.

Serving: This dish should be served in a large communal bowl placed at the centre of the table for the diners to help themselves.

SHALLOW-FRY OF TWO TYPES OF MUSHROOM
Chao Shuang Dong

10 medium Chinese dried
  mushrooms
12 large fresh mushrooms
3½ tablespoons vegetable oil
4 tablespoons stock
1½ tablespoons light soya sauce
1 tablespoon prawn (shrimp) sauce
1 tablespoon cornflour (cornstarch)
  blended with 4 tablespoons
  water

4-5 portions with other dishes

THIS DISH WILL appeal to all mushroom lovers.

Method: Soak dried mushrooms in boiling water for 30 minutes. Remove the stems of both the dried and the fresh mushrooms.

Heat oil in a frying pan. When hot, add the dried mushrooms to shallow-fry over low heat, stem side down for 3 minutes. Add the fresh mushrooms, placing them stem side down, to fry for a further 3 minutes. Add the stock, soya sauce, and prawn sauce. Stir and mix the sauces with the mushrooms for 1 minute. Add the blended cornflour, pouring it evenly over the contents. Stir-fry gently for a further 1½ minutes.

Serving: An attractive way to serve this dish is to decorate the edge of the serving plate with some of the fresh mushroom caps facing downwards. There is a singularly distinct flavour to this dish.

STIR-FRIED GREEN PEAS WITH DRIED AND FRESH PRAWNS (SHRIMPS)

Qing Dou Ha Ren

1½ tablespoons Chinese dried prawns (shrimps)
1 shallot (spring onion/scallion)
2½ tablespoons vegetable oil
2 slices root ginger, shredded
2 cloves garlic, crushed
4 tablespoons fresh or frozen prawns (shrimps), shelled
3 tablespoons stock
375 g (12 oz) fresh or frozen peas
1½ tablespoons light soya sauce
1 tablespoon prawn (shrimp) sauce
1½ teaspoons sesame oil
Salt, to taste
Pepper, to taste

5-6 portions with other dishes

THIS POPULAR DISH is quick to prepare, easy to cook and refreshingly different.

Method: Soak dried prawns in boiling water for 10 minutes. Drain and chop coarsely. Diagonally cut shallot into 2.5 cm (1 in) sections.

Heat the vegetable oil in a wok or non-stick frying pan. When hot, add dried prawns, ginger and garlic. Stir over medium heat for 30 seconds. Add fresh prawns, shallot and stock. When contents come to the boil, stir for a further 15 seconds. Add the peas, sprinkle with soya sauce, prawn sauce and sesame oil. Stir and turn gently until peas are cooked. Season to taste with salt and pepper. Serve.

Serving: This is a very attractive and colourful dish, which can be served with any combination of other savoury dishes and rice.

COLD-TOSSED TOFU (BEANCURD) WITH PICKLES AND DRIED PRAWNS (SHRIMPS)

Ha Mi Zha Cai Ban Doufu

SAUCE

*2 tablespoons Sichuan hot Zha Cai
    pickles, coarsely chopped*
*1½ tablespoons green mustard
    pickles (or Chinese Snow
    Pickles), coarsely chopped*
2 cloves garlic, finely chopped
*3 tablespoons Chinese dried
    prawns (shrimps), soaked for 10
    minutes and finely chopped*
2 teaspoons sugar
*2½ tablespoons rice wine or dry
    sherry*
2½ tablespoons dark soya sauce
*2½ tablespoons fresh lemon juice or
    vinegar*
2½ tablespoons vegetable oil
½ tablespoon sesame oil

3 cakes tofu (beancurd)

5-6 portions as hors d'oeuvre

SERVE AS AN *hors d'oeuvre* or with plain boiled rice.

Method: To make the sauce, combine chopped Zha Cai pickles, green mustard pickles, garlic and chopped dried prawns in a bowl. Add sugar, wine, soya sauce, lemon juice or vinegar, vegetable and sesame oils. Mix them well together. Cut the tofu into 1.5 cm (½ in) cubes.

Serving: Pile tofu cubes on a serving plate. Spoon the sauce over the tofu and toss them lightly together.

HOT-TOSSED TOFU (BEANCURD) WITH MUSHROOMS

Dong Gu Doufu

4 cakes tofu (beancurd)
8 medium fresh mushrooms
3 shallots (spring onions/scallions)
3 tablespoons vegetable oil
1½ tablespoons finely chopped hot
   Sichuan Zha Cai pickles
2½ tablespoons light soya sauce
1 tablespoon Hai Xian (Hoisin)
   sauce
1½ tablespoons Chinese mushroom
   sauce
½ tablespoon chilli sauce
3-4 tablespoons vegetable or meat
   stock
1 teaspoon sugar
1 tablespoon dry sherry

4-6 portions

THIS IS A light, flavoursome dish which can be used as a starter in a long multi-course meal.

Method: Cut each tofu cake into 4-6 pieces. Poach in boiling water for 2 minutes. Lift them out with a perforated spoon, drain and place on a serving dish.

Cut each mushroom into quarters, and shallots into 1 cm (¼ in) diagonal sections. Heat oil in a frying pan. When hot, add mushrooms, shallots and pickles. Stir over medium heat for 1½ minutes. Add all the sauces, stock, sugar and sherry and continue to stir-fry for another 1½ minutes.

Serving: Pour the mushrooms and sauce over the tofu on the serving plate. Toss them lightly together and serve.

TOFU (BEANCURD) WITH SESAME OR PEANUT BUTTER SAUCE

Ma Jiang Doufu

4 cakes tofu (beancurd)
2½ tablespoons sesame paste or
    peanut butter
1 tablespoon sesame oil
1½ tablespoons vegetable oil
3 tablespoons light soya sauce
2 tablespoons cider or wine vinegar
2 shallots (spring onions/scallions)

4-6 portions

I AM INCLUDING this comparatively simple dish as one of China's top dishes mainly because it is evocative of life and eating in China. When there is no great choice of dishes to present for a meal, this should be included on the menu as it will appease hunger and warm the cockles of the heart!

Method: Cut each cake of tofu into 6 cubes, and spread out on a serving dish. Mix the sesame paste or peanut butter with the sesame oil and vegetable oil until well blended. Mix the soya sauce with the cider or vinegar. Diagonally chop the shallots into 1 cm (¼ in) sections.

Serving: Place a dollop of the sesame paste and oil mixture on top of each piece of tofu, and pour a dash of soya sauce and vinegar mixture over them. The diner uses the chopstick to mash or rub the tofu into the soya and vinegar sauce, and the sesame paste, and eats them in conjunction with boiled rice or with Congee.

SICHUAN MA PO TOFU (BEANCURD)

Si Chuan Ma Po Doufu

3-4 cakes tofu (beancurd)
2 tablespoons salted black beans
4 tablespoons vegetable oil
180 g (6 oz) minced pork or beef
Salt, to taste
Pepper, to taste
3 slices root ginger, finely chopped
60 g (2 oz) hot Sichuan Zha Cai
  pickles, finely chopped
3 shallots (spring onions/scallions),
  finely chopped
2 dried chillies (hot peppers)
5 tablespoons stock
2 tablespoons light soya sauce
1 tablespoon chilli sauce
1 tablespoon Sichuan Dou Ban
  (Toupan) chilli paste (optional)
2 tablespoons red or white wine
1 tablespoon cornflour (cornstarch)
  blended with 3 tablespoons
  water
2 teaspoons sesame oil

4-6 portions with other dishes

THIS IS A DISH of the common people. First cooked by a woman who had a pock-marked face — for that is what *Ma Po* means in Chinese — it has always been popular in Japan and is now gaining recognition in the West.

Method: Dice the tofu into sugar lump size cubes. Soak black beans in warm water for 5 minutes, then drain and finely chop.

Heat oil in a wok or a non-stick frying pan. When hot, add the minced meat, salt and pepper and stir-fry over high heat for 2 minutes. Add black beans, ginger, pickles, shallots and chillies and mix together over high heat for another 2 minutes. Add stock, soya sauce, chilli sauce, Dou Ban chilli paste and wine. Stir the mixture into a bubbling sauce. Add the tofu cubes to the sauce, turn them over to take on a thick layer of the sauce. Leave them to cook gently together for a further 3 minutes. Add cornflour mixture, and sesame oil. Stir and turn the contents over medium heat for 1 minute and serve.

Serving: Serve in a deep-sided serving bowl with ample rice. This is a simple dish, but one to be remembered!

RED-COOKED TOFU (BEANCURD) FROM THE FAMILY KITCHEN
Jia Chang Doufu

*120-155 g (4-5 oz) red-cooked pork
  (see page 125)*
3 cakes tofu (beancurd)
*3-4 medium Chinese dried
  mushrooms*
2 medium zucchinis (courgettes)
3 tablespoons vegetable oil
1 medium onion, thinly sliced
2 slices root ginger, shredded
150 mL (¼ pt) stock
3 tablespoons light soya sauce
1 tablespoon oyster sauce
*1 tablespoon Hai Xian (Hoisin)
  sauce*
*45 g (1½ oz) Sichuan Zha Cai
  pickles, finely chopped*
2 teaspoons sugar
*1 tablespoon cornflour (cornstarch)
  blended with 4 tablespoons
  water*

4-5 portions

WE CHINESE ARE fond of using up all the bits and
pieces leftover from previous meals. Hence there are
often "recreated" dishes on the Chinese dining table.
Such dishes are made up of a main ingredient which
is cooked with several leftover ingredients. One
example is Red-Cooked Pork. The flavour of the pork
is enhanced by the dried mushrooms and pickles,
which transform the more neutral tasting ingredients,
such as tofu. This is a very flavoursome dish.

Method: Cut pork into small bite-size pieces. Cut each
piece of tofu into 8 pieces. Soak dried mushrooms in
hot water for 30 minutes. Drain, remove stems and
cut caps into quarters. Cut zucchini diagonally into
1.5 cm (½ in) long segments.
    Heat oil in a wok or non-stick frying pan. When
hot, add onion, ginger and mushrooms. Stir-fry them
over medium heat for 1½ minutes. Add the pork,
zucchinis and tofu. Shallow-fry together for 2½
minutes, turning the contents over. Add the stock,
soya sauce, oyster sauce, Hai Xian sauce, pickles and
sugar. Bring contents to a gentle boil. Simmer for
another 5-6 minutes. Add the blended cornflour. Stir
and turn the contents a few times and serve.

Serving: Serve in a large serving bowl for the diners
to help themselves.

DEEP-FRIED TOFU (BEANCURD) WITH BACON, MUSHROOMS AND EGGS

Yan Rou Doufu

3 cakes tofu (beancurd)
3 eggs
Salt, to taste
250 g (8 oz) fresh mushrooms
1 medium capsicum (sweet pepper)
Oil for deep-frying
2 tablespoons vegetable oil
2 slices bacon, cut into matchsticks
200 mL (⅓ pt) strong stock
1 tablespoon cornflour (cornstarch)
   blended with ¾ tablespoon
   water
1 tablespoon light soya sauce
1½ tablespoons chopped shallots
   (spring onions/scallions)
2 teaspoons sesame oil

5-6 portions with other dishes

THIS IS AN inexpensive, flavoursome dish ideal for a family meal.

Method: Cut each piece of tofu into 6 pieces. Beat eggs lightly with salt. Remove mushroom stems, clean caps and cut each into quarters. Seed and cut capsicum into 1.5 cm (½ in) slices.

Heat oil in a wok or pan and deep-fry the tofu pieces for 2½-3 minutes, drain them and put aside. Heat vegetable oil in a wok. When hot, add bacon and mushrooms, and stir-fry for 2 minutes. Add capsicum and stir-fry for 1 more minute. Pour in the beaten eggs. Stir and turn them gently with the other ingredients over medium heat. When the eggs are about to set, add the deep-fried tofu pieces. Stir and turn them to scramble with the eggs. Pour in the stock, bring to the boil, and turn and stir ingredients together. Simmer over medium heat, stirring several times. Pour the blended cornflour and soya sauce evenly over the contents, and stir and turn them over a couple of times.

Serving: Serve in a well-heated deep-sided bowl, and sprinkle with chopped shallots and sesame oil.

STIR-FRIED TOFU (BEANCURD) WITH SEAFOOD

Hai Xian Doufu

3 cakes tofu (beancurd)
1½ tablespoons Chinese dried
   prawns (shrimps)
3 shallots (spring onions/scallions)
10 medium mussels
3½ tablespoons vegetable oil
3 slices root ginger, shredded
3 slices onion
120 g (4 oz) cooked crabmeat,
   flaked
Salt, to taste
Pepper, to taste
4 tablespoons stock
1½ tablespoons light soya sauce
1 tablespoon oyster sauce
2 tablespoons dry sherry
1 tablespoon cornflour (cornstarch)
   blended with 4 tablespoons
   water

4-6 portions

THIS IS AN extraordinarily savoury dish.

Method: Cut tofu into double sugar lump size pieces. Soak dried prawns in boiling water for 15 minutes, drain and chop coarsely. Chop shallots coarsely dividing the green parts from the white. Clean and poach the mussels in boiling water for 3 minutes. Drain and remove from their shells.

Heat oil in a wok or non-stick frying pan. When hot, add ginger, onion, the white parts of the shallots and the dried prawns. Stir-fry them over medium heat for 1 minute. Add the crabmeat, mussels and tofu. Season with salt and pepper, and stir gently together for 1½ minutes. Add the stock, soya sauce, oyster sauce and sherry. Continue to stir and turn over medium heat for a further 2 minutes. Sprinkle the contents with the blended cornflour and the green of the chopped shallots, stir and turn once more.

Serving: This dish should be eaten hot. Serve on a well-heated plate and accompany with rice.

DISH OF RUNNING YELLOW EGGS
Liu Wang Cai

3 eggs
300 mL (½ pt) strong stock
1½ tablespoons cornflour
*   (cornstarch) blended with 4*
*   tablespoons water*
Salt, to taste
2½ tablespoons vegetable oil
2 teaspoons sesame oil
3 tablespoons green peas

4-5 portions

THIS IS ANOTHER dish typical of Beijing (Peking), which is ladled onto each diner's rice. It adds richness and counteracts the dryness of the rice. Although there are many dishes in China which complement rice, this is the only one which is actually poured on to the rice when eaten.

Method: Break the eggs into a large bowl and beat for 10 seconds. Add the stock, blended cornflour, salt and 2 teaspoons of vegetable oil. Continue to beat for a further 10 seconds until the mixture is well mixed.

  Heat remaining oil in a saucepan. When it is hot, slowly pour in the beaten egg mixture in a thin stream stirring all the time, over low heat. Add the sesame oil and peas and continue to stir and cook slowly until the peas are cooked. The contents in the pan should appear rich, melting and piping hot.

Serving: Pour the contents of the saucepan into a large serving bowl and bring it to the dining table for the diners to help themselves. A warm dish to be tucked into with hot rice, this is very comforting food to have in a Beijing (Peking) winter.

STIR-FRIED OMELETTE WITH TOMATOES
Xian Qie Chao Dan

5 eggs
Salt, to taste
Pepper, to taste
5 medium tomatoes
5 tablespoons vegetable oil
1½ tablespoons soya sauce
2 shallots (spring onions/scallions),
   coarsely chopped

4-5 portions with other dishes

JUST AS THERE is a profusion of Chinese white cabbage in Beijing (Peking) in winter so there is a profusion of tomatoes in the summer. There is little wonder then that tomatoes are frequently used in Chinese dishes. In this recipe the tomatoes are teamed with another food commonly available in the Chinese kitchen: eggs.

Method: Break eggs into a bowl. Add salt and pepper to taste. Beat them until well mixed. Remove the skin of the tomatoes by immersing them in boiling water and cut them into quarters.

Heat oil in a wok or frying pan over medium heat. Tilt the wok so the oil evenly covers the surface. When hot, add the eggs and when they are about to set push them to one side of the wok, and add the tomatoes to the opposite side. When the eggs are completely set, turn and scramble lightly with the tomatoes.

Serving: Sprinkle the contents of the wok with soya sauce, and chopped shallots, and serve. Although a very simple dish, it is often much appreciated by the palates of connoisseurs.

WANG PU MULTI-LAYERED OMELETTE

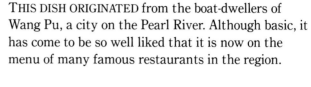

Wang Pu Chao Dan

8 eggs
Salt, to taste
Pepper, to taste
2 tablespoons chopped shallots
   (spring onions/scallions)
125 mL (4 fl oz) vegetable oil
1½ tablespoons rice wine or dry
   sherry
1½ tablespoons light soya sauce

5-6 portions

THIS DISH ORIGINATED from the boat-dwellers of Wang Pu, a city on the Pearl River. Although basic, it has come to be so well liked that it is now on the menu of many famous restaurants in the region.

Method: Break eggs into a bowl. Add salt and pepper to taste and half the chopped shallots. Beat until well mixed.

Heat a third of the oil in a wok or small frying pan. Tilt the wok so the oil evenly covers its surface. Pour in a third of the beaten egg. Before it sets, sprinkle over remaining shallots. When the eggs are about to set completely, transfer the omelette, with the aid of an egg slice to a well-heated serving plate.

Repeat the process by adding and heating the second third of the oil into the now empty wok, followed by pouring in the second third of the beaten egg. When the second omelette has cooked but is still very soft on top, use an egg slice to place it on the serving plate on top of the first omelette. Repeat with the third omelette. When all three omelettes are cooked and in place, sprinkle the top with the combined, heated wine and soya sauce, and the balance of the shallots.

Serving: To be fully appreciated and enjoyed, this dish should be served and eaten with plain boiled rice. Its fascination lies in its interspersed layers of soft and well-cooked eggs flavoured by freshly chopped shallots and wine.

STIR-FRIED EGGS WITH PEPPERED PRAWNS (SHRIMPS)

Ha Yen Chao Dan

5 eggs
Salt, to taste
Pepper, to taste
2 shallots (spring onions/scallions),
    finely chopped
8 prawns (shrimps), shelled
½ teaspoon freshly ground pepper
1 eggwhite, lightly beaten
1 tablespoon cornflour (cornstarch)
6 tablespoons vegetable oil
1 tablespoon rice wine or dry
    sherry

4-5 portions

THOUGH NOT EXACTLY ONE of the most refined dishes, Stir-fried Eggs with Peppered Prawns (Shrimps) is extremely appetizing when eaten with rice.

Method: Beat eggs lightly. Add salt, pepper and shallots. Beat again to fold through. Rub prawns with freshly ground pepper. Wet with eggwhite and dredge in cornflour.

Heat 4 tablespoons oil in a frying pan or wok. When hot, add prawns and stir over medium heat for 1½ minutes; push away from the centre of the heat. Add the balance of the oil to the pan and tilt so the oil evenly covers its surface. Pour in the beaten egg and wait for it to set. As soon as it begins to set bring back the prawns and scramble for 1½ minutes over medium heat.

Serving: Sprinkle the contents of the pan with rice wine or sherry and serve. The alcohol striking the prawns and egg at high heat will release an appetizing aroma.

YELLOW FLOWER PORK

Mu Shu Rou

4 eggs
Salt, to taste
Pepper, to taste
3 tablespoons dry wood ear fungi
4-5 medium Chinese dried
*   mushrooms*
2 shallots (spring onions/scallions)
90 g (3 oz) snow peas (mange tout)
120 g (4 oz) bamboo shoots
120 g (4 oz) pork belly
5 tablespoons vegetable oil
3 tablespoons stock
2 tablespoons dark soya sauce
1 tablespoon rice wine or sherry
1 teaspoon sesame oil

4-5 portions

IT IS PROBABLY true that almost any Chinese stir-fried dish could be combined with eggs to form a new recipe. The best known of these is probably Yellow Flower Pork. It is often served and eaten wrapped in pancakes.

Method: Break eggs into a bowl. Add salt and pepper. Beat well with a fork or a pair of chopsticks. Clean fungi, soak and rinse in warm water for 15 minutes, then drain. Soak dried mushrooms in boiling water for 30 minutes. Drain and cut mushroom caps into quarters. Diagonally cut shallots, snow peas and bamboo shoots into 4 cm (1½ in) sections. Cut pork into thin slices 5 x 2.5 cm (2 x 1 in).

Heat 4 tablespoons of oil in a wok or frying pan. When hot, add the pork and stir-fry over high heat for 2 minutes. Add mushrooms, fungi, snow peas, bamboo shoots and shallots. Stir them together for 3 minutes. Pour the stock and soya sauce over the contents of the wok and stir-fry together for 1½ minutes. Remove the wok from the heat.

Heat remaining oil in a separate wok or pan. When hot, pour in the beaten eggs. Stir a few times, allowing the eggs time to set slowly. When the eggs are set break them up into 2.5-4 cm (1-1½ in) size pieces, and turn them into the wok containing the vegetables. Stir them over medium heat with the pork, vegetables and gravy. Allow the eggs to absorb some of the flavours of the pork and the gravy. Adjust the flavouring by adding rice wine, and sesame oil. Stir-fry gently for a further 30 seconds and serve.

SALT EGGS, SOYA EGGS, TEA EGGS, 100-YEAR-OLD EGGS (1000-YEAR-OLD EGGS)

Xian Dan, Lu Shui Dan, Cha Ye Dan, Pi Dan

YOU COME ACROSS these eggs daily in China. Even when abroad these eggs can be found in the Chinese communities, or in Chinese food shops.

To the Chinese palate, eggs are an ideal complement to rice. These four types of eggs are eaten with Congee — the salty and pickled flavours of the eggs seem to awaken the palate to the sweet and refreshing character of the soft rice.

Salt Eggs: usually larger than normal eggs and pale blue in colour, they are mostly hard-boiled duck eggs which have been soaked in brine for varying lengths of time. When cracked open, the yolk is bright orange. They are usually served cut through the shells into six segments.

Soya Eggs: are hard-boiled eggs that have been cooked in soya sauce, or in the rich gravy of a red-cooked meat dish, such as knuckle of pork, pork trotters, red-cooked beef. After cooking for 30 minutes, the egg will assume a rich dark brown skin, which contrasts perfectly with Congee both in taste and colour.

Tea Eggs: or Marble Eggs are hard-boiled eggs with cracked shells that are soaked, boiled or simmered in strong tea. The tea seeps through the cracks in the shell and produces a marbled pattern on the white of the hard-boiled egg.

100-Year-Old Eggs (1000-Year-Old Eggs): or *Song Hua Dan* or Pine Flower Eggs seem to intrigue Western taste-buds and imaginations: the eggwhite is dark green in colour with a bright yellowish-green yolk. It tastes cheesy and is unmistakably smelly! Always bought in food shops, it is very seldom made at home.

However, here is the recipe. To make a dozen *100-Year-Old Eggs*, dissolve 4 tablespoons sea salt in 450 mL (¾ pt) of water, gradually add 15 tablespoons pine ash and 5 tablespoons lime. Stir them together into a consistent, muddy mixture. Wash the duck eggs in warm water. Coat them completely with .6 cm (¼ in) of the mud pack. Be sure that each egg is completely covered. Roll the mud-covered eggs in a tray of husks or chopped straw, so that they are coated, thus preventing them from sticking to each other. Carefully arrange the eggs in a pile at the bottom of a large earthenware jar. Cover them with a lid.

After three days, take the eggs out and re-arrange them, moving those on the top to the bottom of the pile, and vice versa. Repeat the procedure 5 times in 15 days. After that period of changing and re-arranging, seal the jar by placing the lid on firmly, leaving the eggs to stand undisturbed for one month. After this gestation period of 1½ months, the eggs should be ready for use. The mixture of salt, lime, and ash slowly cooks the eggs and acts as a time-machine shortening the cooking time from a 100 years to 50 days! The eggs, now covered in husks, straw and grey mud, appear remarkably like antique eggs.

Serving: To serve and eat the eggs, wash off the husks, mud and straw under running water, and crack the shells gently. Remove the shells and cut the eggs lengthwise into quarters. In contrast to these eggs, Congee will taste twice as pure and refreshing to the early morning palate.

BASIC STEAMED EGGS

Zheng Shui Dan

3 eggs
450 mL (¾ pt) strong stock
Salt, to taste
1½ tablespoons chopped shallots
   (spring onions/scallions)
1½ tablespoons light soya sauce

4-6 portions

AS MOST SAVOURY dishes in China are cooked to complement rice, a popular way of preparing eggs is to make a savoury custard which blends well with plain boiled rice. When beaten eggs are mixed with water or stock and steamed into a custard, this produces a dish even lighter than scrambled eggs as no oil is used. Many Chinese have fond memories of such a dish as it is often served to the very young, the very old and to invalids.

Method: Beat the eggs with a fork or a pair of chopsticks for 15 seconds. Combine them with the stock and salt. Stir until the mixture is well blended. Pour into a heatproof bowl.

Insert the bowl into a steamer and steam vigorously for 25 minutes. Alternatively place the bowl in 5 cm (2 in) of boiling water at the centre of a saucepan, cover and bring the water in the saucepan to a gentle boil. Allow the contents of the bowl to steam for 20 minutes, when the savoury egg custard should be ready to serve.

Serving: In serving this dish, bring the bowl to the dining table. The top of the custard should now be firm. Sprinkle the top with the chopped shallots and good quality soya sauce. This dish is appealing mainly because of its light and savoury qualities. Many prefer it to the more ordinary stir-fried egg dishes.

FOUR VARIETIES OF STEAMED EGGS
Si Wei Zheng Dan

2 eggs
Salt, to taste
450 mL (¾ pt) stock
1 teaspoon vegetable oil
2 Chinese Salt Eggs
2 Chinese Soya Eggs
2 100-Year-Old Eggs (1000-Year-Old Eggs)
1 Chinese wind-dried sausage or 1 slice bacon
1¼ tablespoons chopped shallots (spring onions/scallions)
1¼ tablespoons light soya sauce

4-5 portions

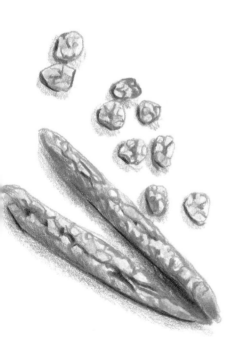

STEAMED SAVOURY EGG custards can be made into more fancy versions simply by blending seafood, flaked fish or minced meat into the beaten eggs and stock before the mixture is steamed in a basin. Such dishes are part of the daily diet of many Chinese.

One of the most interesting fancy steamed savoury egg custards is Four Varieties of Steamed Eggs. In this recipe, Salt Eggs, Soya Eggs and 100-Year-Old Eggs (1000-Year-Old Eggs) are diced and combined with beaten eggs and wind-dried sausage.

Method: Prepare the egg custard mixture in the same manner as in Basic Steamed Eggs. Cut or dice the Salt Eggs, Soya Eggs and 100-Year-Old Eggs into small cubes or segments. Cut the Chinese sausage or bacon into thin slices. Line the bottom of a flat, deep-sided, heatproof dish with the diced egg cubes interspersed with slices of wind-dried sausage. Pour the beaten egg custard mixture over them. Place the heatproof dish in a steamer, or at the bottom of a large saucepan, partly immersed in boiling water, to steam steadily for 20-25 minutes.

Serving: Bring the heatproof dish directly from the steamer to the table. Sprinkle the top of the custard with shallots and soya sauce. The diners help themselves by digging into the savoury custard and adding spoonfuls of the mixed savoury custard on top of their own bowl of rice.

FU RONG CAULIFLOWER

Fu Rong Cai Hua

1 tablespoon Chinese dried prawns
(shrimps)
600 mL (1 pt) stock
Salt, to taste
1 medium cauliflower, in florets
2 tablespoons finely chopped ham

SAUCE

2 eggwhites
150 mL (¼ pt) stock
2 tablespoons minced chicken
breast
Pepper, to taste
2 tablespoons vegetable oil
1½ tablespoons cornflour
(cornstarch) blended with
5 tablespoons milk

4-5 portions

FOR SOME UNSPECIFIED reason, in the west all
Chinese dishes which include eggs are called Fu
Rongs. In China, Fu Rong refers to dishes in which
beaten eggwhite is blended with stock to make a
sauce. Sometimes minced chicken breast, or minced
white fish are added to the beaten eggwhite to make
the Fu Rong dishes richer. In the west, a small
amount of cream may be added to enhance the
richness of the Fu Rong sauce.

Method: Soak dried prawns in hot water for
15 minutes and drain.

Heat stock in a saucepan. Add salt, dried prawns
and cauliflower florets. Bring to the boil and simmer
gently for 8 minutes. Drain.

To make the sauce, beat eggwhites for 10 seconds.
Add the stock, minced chicken and pepper, and beat
together for a further 5-6 seconds. Heat oil in another
saucepan. When hot, add the eggwhite mixture,
stirring in slowly in a thin stream. When the mixture
is coming to the boil, add the cornflour and milk,
which should immediately thicken the sauce.
Continue to turn over low heat for a further
2 minutes.

Serving: Place the cauliflower mixture in a deep bowl.
Pour the sauce over it, and sprinkle with chopped
ham.

FU RONG CHINESE CABBAGE
Fu Rong Bai Cai

2 tablespoons Chinese dried
   prawns (shrimps)
600 mL (1 pt) stock
Salt, to taste
*1 medium Chinese cabbage,
   chopped*
2 tablespoons finely chopped ham

SAUCE

2 eggwhites
150 mL (¼ pt) stock
*2 tablespoons minced chicken
   breast*
Pepper, to taste
2 tablespoons vegetable oil
*1½ tablespoons cornflour
   (cornstarch) blended with
   5 tablespoons milk*

4-5 portions

THE FULL SPLENDOUR of the Chinese cabbage which is grown in profusion in North China in the winter especially around the Beijing (Peking) area can only be appreciated when eaten in quantity. It is the one food which can be fully enjoyed without meat, fish or seafood when consumed with rice.

Method: The cabbage can be cooked in precisely the same manner as cauliflower in the previous recipe, except that when boiling, it will need to be simmered for another 5 minutes with an extra tablespoon of hydrated dried prawns (shrimps) added, and in the serving none of the water used in the boiling needs to be drained away. Otherwise simply follow exactly the same procedure.

Although no meat is employed in the cooking, it seems like a very meaty dish, and is most enjoyable eaten with a large amount of plain rice.

FISH AND SEAFOOD

FISH AND SEAFOOD

CHINA HAS several mighty rivers with thousands of tributaries and a winding coastline more than 4800 kilometres (3000 miles) long. So it is not surprising to discover that fish and seafood are consumed often. This might partly be due to the fact that we have been fish farming since time immemorial: every village in China seems to have a pond or small lake. These are drained once a year and the fully-grown fish are sifted out to be used or sold for food. The smaller fish are returned to the re-flooded ponds to grow for another season.

When cooking fish, we Chinese seldom stir-fry it as it breaks up too easily. Fish is more often steamed, as steam is readily available in a Chinese kitchen, and most fish can be cooked without resorting to the highest temperatures. Fish is also cooked by shallow-frying or pan-frying, followed by lengthier braising. Seafood is often cooked like the small cuts of meat by quick stir-frying.

In the blending and generating of flavours, we Chinese do not feel that the flavours of meat, fish and seafood need to be exclusive of each other. They are often used in conjunction with each other; indeed it is when the two flavours are blended that the most savoury dishes are created.

To reduce the fishy flavour in fish and seafood dishes, we often use ginger and other strong tasting vegetables and herbs. Flavourers such as prawn (shrimp) sauce, or oyster sauce, are seldom used in fish and seafood cookery; this is mainly to avoid doubling up on the fishy flavours. Indeed, in concocting seafood sauces or making fish soups, chicken stock is normally used.

RED-COOKED FISH STEAKS

Hong Shao Yu

700-900 g (1½-2 lb) fish e.g. cod,
   halibut, turbot, bream or
   seabass, cut in large chunks
Salt, to taste
Pepper, to taste
1 eggwhite, lightly beaten
1½ tablespoons cornflour
   (cornstarch)
5 slices root ginger, shredded
5 shallots (spring onions/scallions),
   cut into fine shreds
5 tablespoons vegetable oil

SAUCE

4 tablespoons light soya sauce
2 teaspoons sugar
2 tablespoons stock
2 tablespoons rice wine or dry
   sherry

4-6 portions with other dishes

THESE FISH STEAKS with ginger and onion sauce
make a simple but tasty meal.

Method: Rub the fish with salt and pepper, wet with
eggwhite, and dredge with cornflour. Reserve half the
ginger for the sauce. To make the sauce, mix all
ingredients together until they are well blended.
   Heat oil in a frying pan with a lid. When hot,
sprinkle the oil evenly with chopped ginger, and
arrange the fish on the pan surface. Shallow-fry over
medium heat for 2 minutes, then turn the fish over
with a fish slice to fry on the opposite side for
2 minutes. Drain away any excess oil, and pour in
the sauce. Top with some shallots. Cover and cook
gently for 3 minutes.

Serving: Transfer the fish to a serving plate and pour
sauce from the pan on top of each piece of fish and
sprinkle them with a pinch of shallots.

STEAMED WHOLE FISH

Zhang Yu

*1 whole seabass or bream or any
large firm-fleshed fish weighing
about 2.25 kg (4½ lb)*
Salt, to taste
Pepper, to taste
1 tablespoon vegetable oil
6 shallots (spring onions/scallions)
6 slices root ginger
2 tablespoons light soya sauce
*2 tablespoons rice wine or dry
sherry*
3 tablespoons vegetable oil

7-8 portions with other dishes

THIS RECIPE BRINGS out the full flavour of the fish.

Method: Clean the fish thoroughly. Rub it inside and
out with salt, pepper and oil. Cut the shallots and
ginger into fine double matchsticks. Place the fish
lengthwise on a heatproof oval dish, and over the top
of the fish sprinkle a thick layer of half the shallot
and ginger matchsticks mixed together.

Insert the dish into a preheated steamer to steam
on high heat for 25 minutes. Remove the dish from
the steamer. Brush away the already steamed ginger
and shallot matchsticks from the top of the fish, and
replace with a fresh layer of similar matchsticks.
Pour away half the liquid which has now
accumulated at the bottom of the dish.

Serving: Sprinkle the entire fish with light soya
sauce and rice wine or sherry. Heat the oil until it is
very hot (near boiling) and pour it in a small stream
over the length of the fish through the layer of ginger
shreds and shallots, transferring the flavour of these
strong tasting vegetables to the flesh of the fish.

SICHUAN TOUPAN FISH

Si Chuan Dou Ban Yu

1.25-1.5 kg (2½-3 lb) whole fish
  e.g. seabass, bream, carp or
  trout
Salt, to taste
Pepper, to taste
Oil for deep-frying

SAUCE

2 medium red and green
  capsicums (sweet peppers)
2 tablespoons salted black beans
3 cloves garlic, coarsely chopped
3 slices root ginger, shredded
2 tablespoons vegetable oil
2 medium onions, thinly sliced
2 chillies (hot peppers), finely
  chopped
120 g (4 oz) minced pork
2 tablespoons light soya sauce
4 tablespoons stock
2 teaspoons sugar
2 tablespoons dry sherry
2½ teaspoons Sichuan Dou Ban
  (Toupan) chilli-soya paste

5-6 portions with other dishes

THE SPICINESS OF this fish dish gives it a distinctive Sichuan flavour.

Method: Remove the seeds from the capsicums and cut into 5 x 1 cm (2 x ¼ in) strips. Soak black beans in 4 tablespoons boiling water for 15 minutes, then mash them with the chopped garlic and ginger.

Score the fish on either side with half a dozen deep cuts. Rub with salt and pepper. Fry the fish in hot oil in a deep-fryer for 5-6 minutes or until slightly crisp, then drain and set aside.

To make the sauce, heat the oil in a wok or frying pan. When hot, add the onions to stir-fry for 1 minute. Add the mashed black beans, garlic and ginger, together with the chillies. Stir and mix over high heat for 1½ minutes. Add the minced pork to mix with the other ingredients. Pour in the soya sauce, stock, sugar, sherry and the Dou Ban paste. Cook for 3-4 minutes, stirring now and then. Pour in about 150 mL (¼ pt) boiling water to dilute the contents. Bring to boiling point.

Lay the fish on its full length into the bubbling sauce. Baste the fish with the sauce. Add the strips of capsicum on either side of the fish. Cover the top of the wok and allow the contents to cook gently for 5-6 minutes.

Serving: Transfer the fish to a well-heated serving plate. Spoon the minced pork and other ingredients, including the capsicums, on top of the fish as garnish.

TRIPLE FRY OF THREE DELICIOUSNESS WITH BLACK BEANS

Dou Chi Chao San Xian

150 g (¹/₃ lb) king prawns (large shrimps), shelled and central vein removed

5-6 scallops

90-100 g (3-4 oz) squid or chicken

1¼ tablespoons salted black beans

2 shallots (spring onions/scallions)

½ red capsicum (sweet pepper)

6 tablespoons vegetable oil

3 slices root ginger, shredded

2 cloves garlic, crushed

½ teaspoon chilli sauce

1 tablespoon light soya sauce

5 tablespoons stock

¾ tablespoon cornflour (cornstarch) blended with 3 tablespoons water

1 teaspoon sesame oil

1 tablespoon rice wine

4-5 portions with other dishes

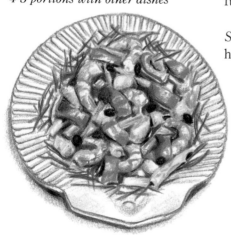

THE THREE MAIN ingredients — prawns, scallops and squid — give this dish its poetic name.

Method: Cut each prawn into 2-3 sections, scallops into halves, and squid or chicken into similar size pieces. Soak black beans in warm water for 10 minutes. Drain and chop coarsely. Cut the shallots diagonally into 2.5 cm (1 in) sections and the capsicum into 2.5 x 1.5 cm (1 x ½ in) pieces.

Heat 4 tablespoons oil in a wok or frying pan. When very hot, add the prawns, scallops and squid or chicken. Stir-fry and turn over high heat for 1½ minutes. Remove with a perforated spoon and set aside. Pour remaining oil into the wok. Add the ginger, garlic and black beans. Stir them over high heat for 30 seconds. Add chilli sauce, soya sauce and stock. Return the prawns, scallops and squid to the wok. Stir into the sauce and turn over high heat for 30 seconds. Sprinkle the contents with blended cornflour, sesame oil and wine. Turn and stir for a further 30 seconds.

Serving: This dish should be served hot on a well-heated plate.

STIR-FRIED KING PRAWNS (LARGE SHRIMPS)
Chao Ha Qiu

375 g (¾ lb) king prawns (large shrimps), shelled and central vein removed
Salt, to taste
½ eggwhite, lightly beaten
1 tablespoon cornflour (cornstarch)
6 tablespoons vegetable oil
3 slices root ginger, shredded
2 cloves garlic, crushed
½ medium onion, very thinly sliced
6 tablespoons stock
1 tablespoon light soya sauce
4-5 tablespoons green peas
1 tablespoon rice wine or dry sherry
1 teaspoon sesame oil
Pepper, to taste
1 tablespoon cornflour (cornstarch) blended with 3 tablespoons water

4-5 portions with other dishes

THIS SAVOURY DISH can be eaten with a wide variety of other dishes, irrespective of their basic flavours. As it is easy and quick to cook, it ranks as one of the most popular party dishes in China.

Method: Wash the prawns. Rub with salt, wet with eggwhite and dredge with cornflour.

Heat 4 tablespoons oil in a wok or frying pan. When hot, add ginger, garlic and onion to stir-fry for 15 seconds. Add prawns and stir-fry over high heat for 1¼ minutes. Remove the prawns with a perforated spoon and set aside. Add stock, soya sauce and peas to the wok. When contents reboil, cook for 3 minutes, stirring from time to time. Return the prawns into the clear bubbling sauce. Sprinkle contents with wine or sherry, sesame oil, pepper to taste and blended cornflour. Turn and stir over high heat for 15 seconds and serve.

CHILLI PRAWNS (SHRIMPS)

La Jiao Ha

500 g (1 lb) king prawns (large shrimps), shelled and central vein removed
Salt, to taste
Pepper, to taste
1 eggwhite, lightly beaten
1½ tablespoons cornflour (cornstarch)
1 tablespoon rice wine or dry sherry
150 mL (¼ pt) oil for frying
1 small green chilli (hot pepper), seeded and chopped
2 small red dried chillies (hot peppers), seeded and chopped
3 slices root ginger, chopped
2 shallots (spring onions/scallions), diagonally chopped
1 tablespoon yellow bean paste
1 tablespoon light soya sauce
1 teaspoon sugar
1½ tablespoons stock
1 tablespoon cornflour (cornstarch) blended with 3 tablespoons water
1 teaspoon sesame oil

4-6 portions with other dishes

THIS IS A SPICY dish, full of zest. Serve as a contrast to the more neutral tasting dishes which often form the general background of a multi-course Chinese dinner.

Method: Rinse prawns under running water and drain well. Place the prawns in a bowl with salt, pepper, eggwhite, cornflour and wine or sherry, and mix them well.

Heat oil in a wok or deep-sided frying pan. When hot, add the prawns to stir and fry over medium heat for 2 minutes. Remove with a perforated spoon, set aside and drain. Pour away most of the oil, leaving 2 tablespoons at the bottom of the wok.

When hot, add the chillies, ginger and shallots, and stir-fry over medium heat for 30 seconds. Add the yellow bean paste, soya sauce, sugar and stock. Stir and mix them together over high heat for 15 seconds. Return the prawns to the bubbling sauce. Continue to stir. Sprinkle the contents with blended cornflour and sesame oil. Stir once more and serve.

SICHUAN CHILLI SQUID

Si Chuan La Jiao You Yu

500 g (1 lb) fresh squid
Salt, to taste
Pepper, to taste
1 small red capsicum (sweet
  pepper)
1 small green capsicum (sweet
  pepper)
3 tablespoons vegetable oil
3 slices root ginger, coarsely
  chopped
3 cloves garlic, coarsely chopped

SAUCE

2 tablespoons vegetable oil
2 tablespoons yellow bean paste
2 tablespoons Sichuan Dou Ban
  (Toupan) chilli-soya sauce
1½ tablespoons light soya sauce
1 tablespoon tomato purée
1½ tablespoons rice wine or dry
  sherry
1 tablespoon cornflour (cornstarch)
  blended with 3 tablespoons
  water

4-6 portions with other dishes

IN THIS DISH the spicy sauce adds the flavour and the squid the texture. The speed with which you cook the squid determines the texture — the longer it is cooked, the more chewy it will be.

Method: Clean squid under running water. Drain and cut into 4 x 2 cm (1½ x ¾ in) strips. Score with criss-cross cuts (cutting in each instance halfway through each strip of squid 6 times). Sprinkle and rub with salt and pepper. Cut the capsicums into the same size pieces as the squid.

Heat oil in a wok or frying pan. When hot, add the ginger and garlic and stir them around a few times. Add the squid and stir over high heat for 1 minute; remove and set aside.

To make the sauce, add oil to the wok. When hot, add yellow bean paste, Sichuan Dou Ban sauce, soya sauce, tomato purée, wine or sherry and blended cornflour. Stir and mix until the sauce thickens. Add the capsicums, and return the squid to the wok. Stir over high heat for 1 minute and serve.

STIR-FRIED EGGS WITH SCALLOPS
Fu Zhou Dai Zi

3 shallots (spring onions/scallions)
4 tablespoons vegetable oil
250 g (½ lb) fresh scallops (shelled)
Salt, to taste
Pepper, to taste
1½ tablespoons rice wine or dry
   sherry
3 eggs, beaten
2 tablespoons finely chopped ham

4-6 portions

AS WITH ALL CHINESE-COOKED seafood meals, this dish should be consumed hot. The last moment addition of chopped shallots enhances the aromatic appeal of the dish.

Method: Chop the shallots finely, dividing the white parts from the green.

Heat 3 tablespoons of oil in a wok or frying pan. When hot, add the scallops and the white of the shallots. Stir-fry them together over medium heat for nearly 1 minute. Add salt, pepper and wine or sherry. Continue to stir-fry them together for a further minute. Remove them from the wok and set aside.

Add remaining oil to the wok. When hot, pour in the beaten eggs. Stir them around a few times, but before they have set, return the scallops to the wok. Sprinkle the contents with the shallot greens and chopped ham. Turn and stir them together for a further 15 seconds, then serve.

CRAB IN HOT BLACK BEAN SAUCE

Chi Jiao Xie

1.25 kg (2½ lbs) fresh crabs
5-6 shallots (spring onions/
*   scallions)*
2 tablespoons salted black beans
3 cloves garlic, finely chopped
5-6 slices root ginger, shredded
2 red chillies (hot peppers), seeded
*   and chopped*
Salt, to taste
1½ tablespoons wine or sherry
5-6 tablespoons vegetable oil
3 tablespoons stock
2 tablespoons vinegar
½ tablespoon sugar
1½ tablespoons light soya sauce
2 eggs, beaten
1 tablespoon cornflour (cornstarch)
*   blended with 3 tablespoons*
*   water*
1½ teaspoons sesame oil

4-5 portions with other dishes

THIS IS AN extremely flavoursome dish. Justice can only be done to it if the fingers are used for eating it.

Method: Scrub and clean crabs under running water. Break or chop each crab into 6-8 pieces, removing the dead men's fingers (the gills). Crack the claws and legs with the back and side of the cleaver. Cut shallots into 1 cm (½ in) sections. Soak the black beans in hot water for 5 minutes, and then drain, chop and crush. Place the crab pieces in a large bowl with half the garlic, shallots, ginger, chillies, salt, wine or sherry and black beans. Mix them all together and leave them to marinate for 30 minutes.

Heat oil in a wok or pan. When very hot, add the crab pieces to stir-fry over high heat for 3½ minutes. Remove and drain. Pour away any excess oil, leaving about 1½ tablespoons in the wok. Reheat; when hot add the remaining black beans, shallots, garlic and chillies; stir over medium heat for 45 seconds. Add the stock, vinegar, sugar and soya sauce. When contents boil, return the crab pieces to the wok and stir over high heat for 2 minutes. Add the beaten eggs, pouring evenly over the contents. When the eggs set, sprinkle the contents with the blended cornflour and sesame oil. Turn and stir once more until the sauce thickens. Serve.

CANTONESE ONION AND GINGER LOBSTER

Jiang Cong Long Ha

*1 lobster weighing about 700 g
    (1½ lb)*
2 shallots (spring onions/scallions)
2 slices root ginger
1½ tablespoons rice wine

DIP SAUCE

2 shallots (spring onions/scallions)
2 slices root ginger
2 chillies (hot peppers)
2½ tablespoons vegetable oil
3 tablespoons light soya sauce
2 tablespoons wine vinegar
1 teaspoon sesame oil

3-4 portions with other dishes

THIS IS AN IDEAL recipe for those who prefer to have plainly cooked fresh lobster.

Method: Wash and clean the lobster under running water. Cut lengthwise into halves, discarding the stomach and intestinal vein. Further cut lobster into 5 cm (2 in) sections. Mix the finely chopped shallots and ginger with the wine. Sprinkle the mixture on top of the lobster pieces. Arrange lobster pieces on a heatproof dish.

Place the heatproof dish in a steamer and steam vigorously for 10 minutes.

To prepare the dip sauce, finely chop the shallots, ginger and chillies, and arrange in a heatproof bowl. Heat the oil in a small pan until smoking hot. Pour it over the contents of bowl and stir together. Pour in the soya sauce, vinegar and sesame oil. Mix them well together and serve.

Serving: The dip sauce should be served on the table with the steamed lobster.

PEKING SLICED FISH IN WINE-LEE SAUCE

Jiu Liu Yu Pian

250 g (½ lb) fillet of sole, halibut or
    flounder
Salt, to taste
1 eggwhite, lightly beaten
1½ tablespoons cornflour
    (cornstarch)
60 g (2 oz) wood ear fungi
Oil for deep-frying
2 slices root ginger

SAUCE

5 tablespoons chicken stock
1½ teaspoons sugar
3 tablespoons white wine
1 teaspoon vodka
½ tablespoon cornflour (cornstarch)
    blended with 2½ tablespoons
    water

4-5 portions with other dishes

THE CLEAN WHITENESS of the fish contrasts well
with the jet black wood ears in the translucent sauce
— a refined dish much seen on dining tables in
Beijing (Peking).

Method: Cut fish into 4 x 2.5 cm (1½ x 1 in) slices.
Rub with salt, wet with eggwhite and dredge with
cornflour. Soak wood ears in hot water for 10 minutes
and drain.

Heat oil in a wok or deep-sided frying pan.
When hot, reduce the heat to low and lay the slices of
fish evenly in the oil to poach for 2 minutes, turning
them over once. Remove the fish with a fish slice, set
aside and drain. Pour away the oil, leaving 2
tablespoons in the wok. Return wok to heat. Add
ginger to flavour the oil, and remove after 30 seconds.
Add wood ears and stir in the oil for 30 seconds.

To make the sauce, combine all ingredients and
pour into the wok. Stir over medium heat until the
sauce thickens. Return the fish slices to the wok and
cook in the sauce, for 1½ minutes.

Serving: To serve, transfer the contents on to a well-
heated serving plate.

"SQUIRREL" FISH

Song Shu Yu

1 whole fish weighing about
    700-900 g (1½-2 lb)
Salt, to taste
Pepper, to taste
4 slices root ginger, finely chopped
3 tablespoons cornflour (cornstarch)
Oil for deep-frying

SAUCE

5 medium Chinese dried
    mushrooms
3 tablespoons wood ear fungi
3 shallots (spring onions/scallions)
2 tablespoons vegetable oil
60 g (2 oz) bamboo shoots, chopped
1 slice bacon, finely chopped
3 tablespoons soya sauce
3 tablespoons stock
2 tablespoons vinegar
1½ teaspoons sugar
2 tablespoons rice wine
1 tablespoon cornflour (cornstarch)
    blended with 4 tablespoons
    water

8-10 portions with other dishes

THIS IS FREQUENTLY served at dinner parties.

Method: Clean the fish and dry well. Cut and slit open from head to tail on the underside. Cut 7-8 deep slashes on one side of the fish, and only two similar slashes on the other side. Rub fish inside and out with salt, pepper and ginger; coat with cornflour. Soak mushrooms and wood ear fungi separately in hot water for 25 minutes. Drain the wood ears and chop finely. Remove the tough stems from the mushrooms and cut caps into thin slices. Cut shallots diagonally into 5 cm (2 in) sections.

Heat oil in a wok or deep-fryer. When hot, gently lower the fish to deep-fry for 3½-4 minutes. Reduce heat to low.

To make the sauce, heat vegetable oil in a wok or frying pan, add wood ears, dried mushrooms, bamboo shoots, bacon and shallots. Stir-fry them over medium heat for 1¼ minutes. Add soya sauce, stock, vinegar, sugar, wine and cornflour. Stir together for a further 1 minute.

While the sauce is cooking, raise the heat of the oil in which the fish is being cooked in order to crisp the fish. Ensure that the fish is placed with the side cut twice facing up, to enable the traditional curling of the tail. When this happens, lift the fish out of the hot oil to drain and place it on a well-heated serving plate. Raise the heat under the pan in which the sauce is being cooked. As the sauce bubbles pour it over the crispy fish. At this point the fish will still be so hot that it will sizzle when the sauce is being poured over it. The fish appears therefore to "chatter" when it is being brought to the table.

SWEET AND SOUR FISH

Tian Suan Yu

250 g (½ lb) fillet of fish
Salt, to taste
½ medium each of red and green
    capsicums (sweet peppers)
1 slice pineapple
Oil for deep-frying
1 slice root ginger
1 small onion, thinly sliced
2 tablespoons vegetable oil

BATTER

1 egg
3 tablespoons plain flour
2 tablespoons self-raising flour
Salt, to taste
Milk

SAUCE

2 tablespoons sugar
3 tablespoons vinegar
3 tablespoons orange juice
1½ tablespoons tomato purée
1 tablespoon cornflour (cornstarch)
    blended with 3 tablespoons
    water

5-6 portions with other dishes

THE MOST POPULAR sweet and sour fish meal in China is made from Yellow River Carp, but carp contains too many bones for the average Westerner. Use instead a more easily manageable fish such as cod, halibut, haddock, sole or plaice.

Method: Cut fish into 5 x 4 cm (2 x 1½ in) pieces. Rub them with salt. Mix the ingredients for the batter adding sufficient milk to make it smooth. Dip the pieces of fish in the batter. Cut the capsicum halves into pieces half the size of the fish, and the pineapple into 4 cm (1½ in) wedges. Mix the sauce ingredients together until smooth.

Heat oil in a wok or deep-fryer. Test heat by dropping in the piece of ginger — when hot it will sizzle. Add the fish, piece by piece and fry for 2 minutes over medium heat. Remove the fish with a slotted spoon and drain.

Heat vegetable oil in a separate wok or frying pan. When hot, add onion slices and stir them for 30 seconds. Pour in the sauce and stir until it thickens. Add the fish pieces, spreading them out evenly over the wok. Turn them lightly over in the sauce and cook them gently for 2 minutes. Serve.

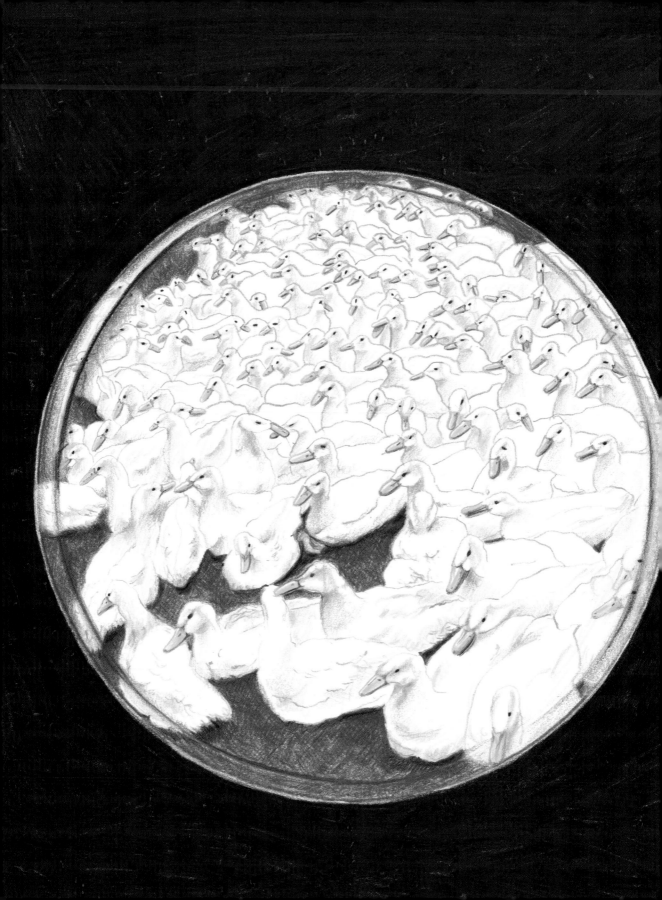

CHICKEN AND DUCK

CHICKEN AND DUCK

ONCE, CHICKEN WAS second to pork as the most widely used meat in Chinese cooking. In recent years it has overtaken pork in the order of popularity, due to its cheap price and also because it is more readily available. As well, chicken possesses the same neutral savouriness as pork, and in Chinese cooking it is easily cooked and blended with other items of food, to produce innumerable dishes.

In Chinese cooking and food presentation, dishes cannot be conveniently divided into appetizers, starters and main courses. Nearly all stir-fried dishes can be served and classified as appetizers/starters. Perhaps only the large stewed and whole roasted meat and fish dishes, which are eaten with rice or noodles, can be classified as main courses. Accordingly, in writing and structuring this chapter on chicken and duck dishes I shall start with a quick run-through of the stir-fried and lighter dishes.

Duck appears on the table less frequently than chicken, but it is easily the second most widely eaten fowl in China. The numerous streams, canals, rivers, lakes, and water-ways of China produce unlimited numbers of lively flocks of ducks every season, which almost equal the number of chickens that peck around the farmyards in their twos and threes. Being a stronger-tasting meat, duck is considered more special than chicken.

WHITE CUT CHICKEN
Bai Qie Ji

1.75-2 kg (3½-4 lb) young chicken
2.2 L (4 pt) water
4 slices root ginger
Salt, to taste

SAUCE

3-4 tablespoons dark soya sauce
2 tablespoons wine vinegar
1½ teaspoons chilli sauce
*2 tablespoons shallots (spring
   onions/scallions), finely chopped*
3 cloves garlic, finely chopped
1 chilli (hot pepper), finely chopped
2 teaspoons vegetable oil
1½ teaspoons sesame oil

5-8 portions

SERVE THIS AS a starter dish at a dinner party.

Method: Clean the chicken thoroughly. Bring water to the boil in a heavy saucepan. Add the ginger, salt and chicken to the boiling water. When contents reboil, lower the heat to a simmer and cook gently for 1 hour or until done, turning the bird over a couple of times. Turn the heat off completely, cover, and allow the chicken to stand and cool in the stock for 30 minutes, before refrigerating.
   To make the sauce, mix the ingredients in a jug until well blended.

Serving: When the chicken is cool, remove from the stock. Reserve stock for some other purpose. Place chicken on a heavy chopping board and chop it into 5 x 4 cm (2 x 1½ in) double-mahjong size pieces. Reassemble the chicken pieces on a large serving dish roughly into the shape of a chicken. Pour the sauce evenly over the chicken and serve.

SHANGTUNG HAND-SHREDDED CHICKEN

Shan Dong Shou Si Ji

*1 young roasting chicken weighing
    about 1.75-2 kg
    (3½-4 lb)*
2 medium sticks of celery, chopped
4 slices root ginger, chopped
*½ medium red capsicum (sweet
    pepper), chopped*
*2 medium chillies (hot peppers),
    chopped*
*4-5 thin slices of Zha Cai pickles,
    chopped*
*3 shallots (spring onions/scallions),
    chopped*
Salt, to taste
3 cloves garlic, crushed

SAUCE

2 tablespoons light soya sauce
1 tablespoon wine vinegar
1½ tablespoons vegetable oil
1½ teaspoons sesame oil
2 tablespoons stock

*6-10 portions with other dishes
    for a party*

THIS DISH IS very tasty and easy to prepare.

Method: Roast the chicken in an oven preheated to
200°C (400°F/Gas mark 6) for 1½ hours. When cool,
cut into small pieces and shred. To make the sauce,
mix the ingredients together until well blended.

Serving: Mix and toss together all the ingredients on
a serving platter. Sprinkle with salt and garlic.
Pour over the sauce and serve as a starter.

DRUNKEN CHICKEN

Zui Ji

1 small young chicken weighing
  about 1.6 kg (3½ lb)
1.8 L (3 pt) water
Salt, to taste
2 medium onions, sliced
4-5 slices root ginger
600 mL (1 pt) rice wine or dry
  sherry
2 tablespoons shallots (spring
  onions/scallions), finely chopped

8-10 portions with other dishes

IF SERVING AT a cocktail party as finger-food, remove the chicken bones or use chicken breast instead.

Method: Clean and truss the chicken. Bring water to the boil in a deep saucepan. Add salt, onions and ginger. Boil for 5 minutes. Add the chicken. Bring to the boil again. Reduce heat and simmer gently for 50 minutes. Turn off the heat, cover and stand on the stove for another 25 minutes. Place in the refrigerator for 3 hours.

Drain completely. Place in a bowl. Pour in the wine or sherry. Turn chicken over several times to ensure that it is covered in wine. Place in the refrigerator for 18 hours, turning the bird every 6 hours.

Serving: Drain and untruss the chicken. Chop into 5 x 4 cm (2 x 1½ in) fricassée or double-mahjong size pieces. Arrange on a large serving plate, sprinkle with shallots, and decorate by surrounding the chicken with flowers. Serve as an *hors d'oeuvre*.

PAPER-WRAPPED CHICKEN
Zhi Bao Ji

4-5 medium Chinese dried
  mushrooms
1 large chicken breast weighing
  about 250 g (½ lb)
3-4 broccoli spears
2 shallots (spring onions/scallions)
Cellophane or oven bags
Salt, to taste
Pepper, to taste
1 teaspoon sugar
1 teaspoon vegetable oil
1 tablespoon light soya sauce
¾ tablespoon Hai Xian (Hoisin)
  sauce
1 tablespoon dry sherry
Oil for deep-frying

4-6 portions with other dishes

FOR THIS RECIPE it is essential to use non-plastic
Cellophane, as the plastic type will shrivel and burn
on contact with the hot oil.

Method: Soak dried mushrooms in 300 mL (½ pt) of
boiling water for 1 hour. Remove the stalks and cut
caps into thin slices. Cut chicken into thin pieces.
Blanch broccoli in boiling water for 2 minutes and
break into individual florets. Cut shallots diagonally
into 4 cm (1½ in) sections. Cut Cellophane or oven
bags into 15 x 10 cm (6 x 4 in) pieces. Rub the
chicken with salt, pepper, sugar and oil, and
refrigerate for 20 minutes. Add the vegetables and
sprinkle with soya sauce, Hai Xian sauce and sherry.
Turn the vegetables over to mix with the chicken.
  Use a large spoon to scoop up roughly
2 tablespoons of the chicken and vegetable mixture
and place it just below the centre of a piece of
Cellophane. Fold the bottom edge up to cover the
ingredients and turn the two sides in. Finally, fold
the top edge down and tuck in. Press each envelope
flat and pile them up as they are made.
  Heat oil for deep-frying. When very hot, carefully
lower in 3 or 4 envelopes at a time. Fry for 2½-3
minutes. Remove and drain on absorbent paper.

Serving: When all the stuffed envelopes have been
fried, arrange them on a flat warmed plate. The food
inside the envelopes is somewhat insulated and
should be still cooking after 3-4 minutes. Open the
packages with the aid of chopsticks.
  This is an ideal dish for a party or banquet.

LEMON CHICKEN

Ning Meng Ji

375 g (12 oz) chicken breast
Salt, to taste
Pepper, to taste
1 teaspoon vegetable oil for rubbing
    on chicken
3 shallots (spring onions/scallions)
3½ tablespoons vegetable oil for
    stir-frying
3 slices root ginger, chopped into
    double matchsticks
Rind of 1½ medium lemons,
    chopped into double matchsticks
1 medium red capsicum (sweet
    pepper), thinly sliced
1 medium green capsicum (sweet
    pepper), thinly sliced
3 tablespoons stock
2 tablespoons dry sherry
3 tablespoons light soya sauce
Juice from 2 medium lemons

4-5 portions with other dishes

THE SHARP, FRESH flavour of this dish is essential to its success — hence the late application of the lemon juice, which should not be cooked for any prolonged length of time.

Method: Cut chicken meat into 4 x 1 cm (1½ x ¼ in) slices. Rub chicken with salt, pepper and oil. Chop shallots diagonally into 4 cm (1½ in) sections.

Heat the oil in a wok or frying pan. When hot, add ginger, chicken and lemon rind. Stir-fry over high heat for 2 minutes. Remove and set aside.

Add shallots and capsicums. Stir-fry over high heat. Pour in the stock, sherry and soya sauce. When contents boil, return the chicken to the wok and toss in the sauce. After 1½ minutes, or when the liquid in the wok reduces by half, sprinkle with freshly squeezed lemon juice. Turn the contents just once more over high heat and serve.

PEKING CHICKEN IN SOYA PASTE SAUCE
Gong Bao Ji Ding

500 g (1 lb) boned chicken breast
Salt, to taste
1 eggwhite, lightly beaten
1½ tablespoons cornflour
   (cornstarch)
4 tablespoons cashew nuts
3½ tablespoons vegetable oil
3 slices root ginger
1½ teaspoons sesame oil

SAUCE

1½ tablespoons yellow bean sauce
1½ tablespoons dark soya sauce
1 tablespoon Hai Xian (Hoisin)
   sauce
2 teaspoons sugar
¾ tablespoon cornflour (cornstarch)
   blended with 2 tablespoons
   water

5-6 portions with other dishes

THIS IS A VERY traditional Beijing (Peking) dish, which carries a great deal of the flavour of China's old capital.

Method: Dice chicken into 1.5 cm (½ in) size cubes. Rub with salt, wet with eggwhite and dredge with cornflour. Heat the nuts in a dry pan, stir until crisp and slightly brown, and put aside. To make the sauce, mix all the ingredients until well blended.

Heat the vegetable oil in a wok or frying pan. Add the ginger and stir for 1 minute to flavour the oil. When the oil is very hot, add the chicken cubes and spread them to shallow-fry evenly. After 1 minute turn the chicken cubes over and stir-fry for another 45 seconds. Push chicken away from the heat. Pour in the sauce and stir over medium heat until the sauce thickens. Return chicken cubes and stir-fry in the sauce over high heat for 45 seconds. Add the crisp nuts and the sesame oil. Continue to stir-fry for 30 seconds and serve.

CHICKEN IN VINEGAR SAUCE

Cu Liu Ji

315 g (10 oz) boned chicken breast
90 g (3 oz) bamboo shoots
Salt, to taste
1 eggwhite, lightly beaten
1 tablespoon cornflour (cornstarch)
4 tablespoons vegetable oil
1 medium onion, thinly sliced
1 clove garlic, chopped
2 slices root ginger, chopped
1 dried chilli (hot pepper), chopped

SAUCE

1 tablespoon cornflour, (cornstarch)
   blended with 3 tablespoons
   water
3 tablespoons wine vinegar
1½ tablespoons light soya sauce
1½ tablespoons stock
1 tablespoon dry sherry

4-6 portions with other dishes

THIS DISH IS enjoyed in Beijing (Peking) by people who appreciate the contrast of pronounced flavours. Here the sharp sour flavour of the vinegar in the sauce is contrasted with the uncomplicated flavour of the lightly salted chicken.

Method: Dice the chicken and bamboo shoots into 1.5 cm (½ in) cubes. Sprinkle chicken with salt, wet with eggwhite and dredge with cornflour. To make sauce, mix all ingredients until well blended.

Heat 3 tablespoons vegetable oil in a wok or frying pan. When hot, add the diced chicken cubes and the bamboo shoots. Stir-fry over high heat for 2 minutes, remove from pan and set aside.

Add remaining oil to the pan. When hot, add onion, garlic, ginger and chilli. Stir them over high heat for 1 minute. Pour in the sauce and stir until it thickens. Return the chicken and bamboo shoots to the pan. Stir-fry for 1 minute and serve.

RED-COOKED CHICKEN

Hong Shao Ji Jian

1 chicken weighing about 2 kg
  (4 lb)
4 tablespoons vegetable oil
2 medium onions, thinly sliced
4 slices root ginger, chopped
6-6½ tablespoons dark soya sauce
6-6½ tablespoons rice wine or dry
  sherry
600 mL (1 pt) stock or water
3 teaspoons sugar

6-8 portions

RED-COOKED DISHES ARE the basic Chinese stews.
Meat and chicken, and in a number of cases
vegetables, are stewed with soya sauce. It is a very
simple form of cooking which is widely used in China
especially when there are many mouths to feed and
there is ample food available. It produces large
quantities of very appealing gravy which, if eaten
with even greater quantities of rice, should give a
great deal of satisfaction to a large number of people.

Method: Chop the chicken into 20-24 5 x 4 cm
(2 x 1½ in) double-mahjong size pieces.
  Heat oil in a casserole or heavy saucepan.
When hot, add onions and ginger and stir them
together over medium heat for 2 minutes. Add the
chicken pieces and turn in the hot oil for 3-4 minutes.
Add soya sauce, wine or sherry, stock or water, and
sugar. Bring contents to the boil. Reduce heat to low
and simmer gently for 1 hour and 10 minutes. Turn
over the contents every 15 minutes. Add a little more
water or stock if the contents become too thick or
dry after the first hour.
  After just over an hour's cooking the chicken
should be well cooked. Serve.

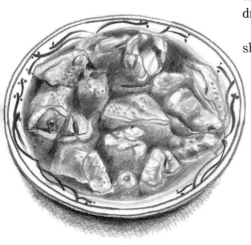

SHANGHAI SOYA AND GINGER GLAZED CHICKEN

Shang Hai Jiang Jiang Ji

1 chicken weighing about 2 kg
  (4 lb)
3 tablespoons vegetable oil
5 slices root ginger
2 medium onions, thinly sliced
5 tablespoons rice wine or dry
  sherry
1½ tablespoons sugar
3½ tablespoons dark soya sauce
2½ tablespoons yellow bean paste
2 tablespoons Hai Xian (Hoisin)
  sauce
450 mL (¾ pt) chicken stock

GARNISH

1 shallot (spring onion/scallion),
  finely chopped or coriander
  leaves

6-8 portions with other dishes

QUICK STIR-BRAISING could probably be used to describe the unnamed process of cooking this dish.

Method: Chop chicken into large bite-size pieces. Cook in a saucepan half-filled with boiling water for 5-6 minutes, then drain.

Heat oil in a large wok or a deep frying pan. Add ginger and onions. Stir-fry over medium heat for 3-4 minutes. Add the chicken pieces and all the remaining ingredients, reserving the garnish. Raise the heat to high. The contents should soon boil and bubble.

Continue cooking on high heat for 20-25 minutes turning the chicken as the stock reduces. The sauce should have now thickened to a glaze. Reduce the heat to prevent the sauce burning. When the pieces of chicken begin to shine like glass, the coating has become more of a glaze than a sauce. This is when the dish is ready to serve.

Serving: Garnish with a sprinkle of chopped shallots or sprays of coriander leaves.

SALT-BURIED CRISPY CHICKEN
Yan Hong Ji

*1 young chicken weighing about
    2 kg (4 lb)
2.5-3 kg (5-6 lb) coarse sea salt*

8-10 portions with other dishes

THERE ARE MANY different recipes for Crispy Chicken in Chinese cuisine. This is probably the most interesting way to prepare it for a banquet.

Method: Wash and dry the chicken thoroughly, cover loosely and refrigerate overnight. Heat salt in a heatproof casserole over low heat for 10-15 minutes. When the salt is quite hot, form a depression and bury the chicken in it completely. Cover the casserole and place it over low heat for 10 minutes. Transfer the casserole to a preheated oven at 190°C (375°F/Gas mark 6) for 1½ hours.

Serving: Remove the chicken from the salt. When the salt is first brushed off the top of the chicken, the latter will appear surprisingly brown. Place it on a chopping board, and chop it through the bone into 5 x 4 cm (2 x 1½ in) fricassée or double-mahjong size pieces. Pile them up on a well-heated serving plate and serve.
   Note: the salt may be used again.

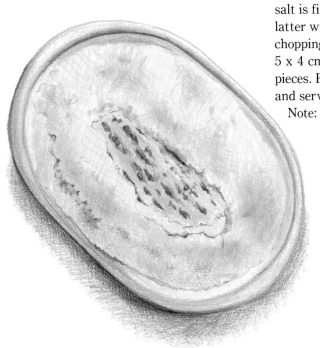

PEKING DUCK

Beijing Kao Ya

2.5-2.75 kg (5-5½ lb) young duck
10-12 shallots (spring onions/
　scallions) cut in 5 cm (2 in)
　shreds
1 medium cucumber, cut in
　matchsticks

PANCAKES

500 g (1 lb) plain flour
1½ teaspoons sugar
1 teaspoon oil
250 mL (8 fl oz) warm water
sesame oil for glazing

SAUCE

3 tablespoons yellow bean paste
3 tablespoons sugar
2 tablespoons vegetable oil
2 teaspoons sesame oil

ALTERNATIVE SAUCE

2 tablespoons Hai Xian (Hoisin)
　sauce
2 tablespoons plum sauce
1 tablespoon dark soya sauce
1 tablespoon vegetable oil
½ tablespoon sesame oil

6-8 portions

THE MOST FAMOUS duck dish in China is Peking Duck. Strangely enough it is probably also one of the easiest to cook. Indeed it is easier to cook in the average Western kitchen than in Beijing (Peking) itself. Peking Duck is a roast duck which has to be cooked in an oven, and hardly any Chinese kitchen has an oven, and therefore cannot be cooked at home. In Beijing, Peking Duck is only available in specialised restaurants (all the top-line duck restaurants in Beijing prepare and serve nearly a thousand ducks a day) while in Europe, America and Australia, the dish can be prepared and cooked in most kitchens. The principal aim in preparing Peking Duck is to produce a duck dish where the bird's skin is distinctly crispy; this is carved off first and eaten together with thin slices of meat, which are wrapped in a pancake with shredded shallots and cucumber, and doused with a sweet, fruity soya-paste sauce. It is the combination of these contrasting flavours and textures which give the dish its distinctive character and endows it with its enduring appeal.

Method: Clean the duck inside and out and lower it momentarily into a pan of boiling water for a quick scald of 8-10 seconds. Drain well, and wipe with several changes of paper towel to dry thoroughly. Cover loosely and refrigerate overnight. By the next day the skin of the bird should be sufficiently dry for it to be roasted in the oven.

Preheat the oven to 200°C (400°F/Gas mark 6). Place duck on the top rack with a roasting pan underneath to catch any fluid. Roast for 1 hour or until the duck is well cooked and the skin very crispy. Place shallots and cucumber in small individual dishes for the diners to help themselves.

To make the pancakes, sift the flour into a mixing bowl. Stir in the sugar, oil and water with a pair of chopsticks or a wooden spoon until well mixed. Knead the mixture into a firm dough, then form 2 large "sausage" strips. Cut each strip into 10 or 12 pieces and form each piece into a small ball. Flatten each ball into a round disc. Brush the top of one of the discs with oil, and place a second disc on top to form a "sandwich". Using a small rolling pin, roll the "sandwich" into a pancake of about 15 cm (6 in) in diameter. Repeat until you have used up all the dough balls and made them into "sandwich" pancakes.

Heat a dry frying pan over low/medium heat. When hot place a "sandwich" pancake on the pan, and shake so that the pancake doesn't stick to the surface of the pan. After 1½ minutes turn the pancake over and cook the other side until the pancake begins to puff and bubble slightly. The pancake is ready when some brown spots begin to appear on the underside. Now very gently peel the "sandwich" apart into its two constituent pancakes. Fold each pancake in half, and stack them up. If they are not used immediately, cover with a damp cloth. They can be reheated in a steamer for a couple of minutes, if necessary.

To make either sauce, combine all ingredients in a small pan and stir over low heat until smooth.

Serving: Cut the skin of the duck into 4-5 cm (1½-2 in) slices with a sharp knife and serve on a heated dish. Slice the meat off the duck into similar sized pieces and serve on a separate heated dish.

Diners help themselves by spreading sauce lavishly over the duck skin and meat, sandwiched inside a pancake with shredded shallots and cucumber.

CRISPY AND AROMATIC DUCK

Xiang Cui Ya

2 kg (4 lb) duck

SEASONING

Salt, to taste
Freshly ground pepper, to taste
¾ teaspoon five spice powder
5 slices root ginger
5 shallots (spring onions/scallions)
4 cloves garlic

MARINADE

3 tablespoons light soya sauce
2 tablespoons vinegar
1½ tablespoons honey

6-8 portions with other dishes

CRISPY AND AROMATIC DUCK has the same appeal as Peking Duck. First and foremost, it is meant to be crispy. In the last stage of cooking it is deep-fried, so its meat and skin are crispier than those of Peking Duck.

Method: Clean the duck thoroughly, inside and out. Combine the salt, pepper and five spice powder. Rub the mixture over the duck, then rub over the finely chopped ginger, shallots and garlic. Cover loosely with aluminium foil, refrigerate and leave the duck to season for 2 hours.

To make the marinade, combine all the ingredients and rub evenly over the duck. Wrap the duck in aluminium foil and place it in a refrigerator to marinate overnight.

After marinating overnight the duck is ready to be cooked, first by steaming, then by deep-frying. The long period of steaming cooks the meat and steams away any excess fat and seasoning; the short period of deep-frying crisps the outer skin.

To steam the duck, remove the foil, place in a steamer and cook for 50-55 minutes. Remove from the steamer and cool.

When cool, double deep-fry the duck for a total of 10-11 minutes: that is, deep-fry twice for 5-6 minutes each, with a break of about 5 minutes between the two sessions of deep-frying.

Serving: To serve this dish, scrape the meat and skin of the duck off the bones. Diners help themselves by wrapping duck in pancakes, with shredded vegetables, and liberally spreading with a piquant sauce. (For the pancake and sauce recipes, see Peking Duck on page 116.)

CANTONESE ROAST DUCK

Shao Ya

2-2.5 kg (4-5 lb) duck
Salt, to taste
2 tablespoons vegetable oil
3 tablespoons chopped onion
2 shallots (spring onions/scallions),
    chopped diagonally into 2.5 cm
    (1 in) pieces
3 tablespoons chopped parsley
2 cloves garlic, crushed
1½ teaspoons crushed peppercorns
150 mL (¼ pt) stock
3 tablespoons soya sauce
2 tablespoons dry sherry
1 tablespoon sugar
½ teaspoon five spice powder
2 tablespoons honey
1½ tablespoons vinegar
150 mL (¼ pt) boiling water
1½ teaspoons cornflour
    (cornstarch) blended with 2
    tablespoons water

5-6 portions with other dishes

THIS IS THE DUCK which is most often seen hanging in Chinese restaurants or shop windows.

Method: Wash the duck under running water and dry thoroughly. Tie the neck tightly with string, so that no liquid will drip out. Refrigerate for 2 hours, then rub it generously inside and out with salt.

Heat oil in a small saucepan. Add chopped onion, shallots, parsley, garlic and peppercorns. Stir-fry for 2 minutes. Pour in the stock. Bring to the boil and simmer gently for 5-6 minutes. Add soya sauce, sherry, sugar and five spice powder, and blend well. Pour this mixture inside the duck and sew up carefully. Secure with skewers so no liquid leaks out. In a separate bowl mix honey and vinegar with boiling water and use for basting the duck.

Preheat the oven to 200°C (400°F/Gas mark 6). Roast the duck on a rack (or hang the duck inside the oven tailside up) for 15 minutes. Baste the duck with the honey-vinegar mixture. Place the bird back in the oven to roast at the reduced heat of 190°C (375°F/Gas mark 5) for 1 hour basting at 30 minute intervals. After the second basting, roast the duck for a further 30 minutes or until cooked.

Remove the bird from the oven to cool for a minute or two. Then carefully remove the strings and skewers, and pour the liquid from the bird's cavity into a pan. Stir in the blended cornflour and bring to the boil. The mixture can be used as sauce.

Serving: As this dish is rich, it is best served with rice and plain cooked vegetables.

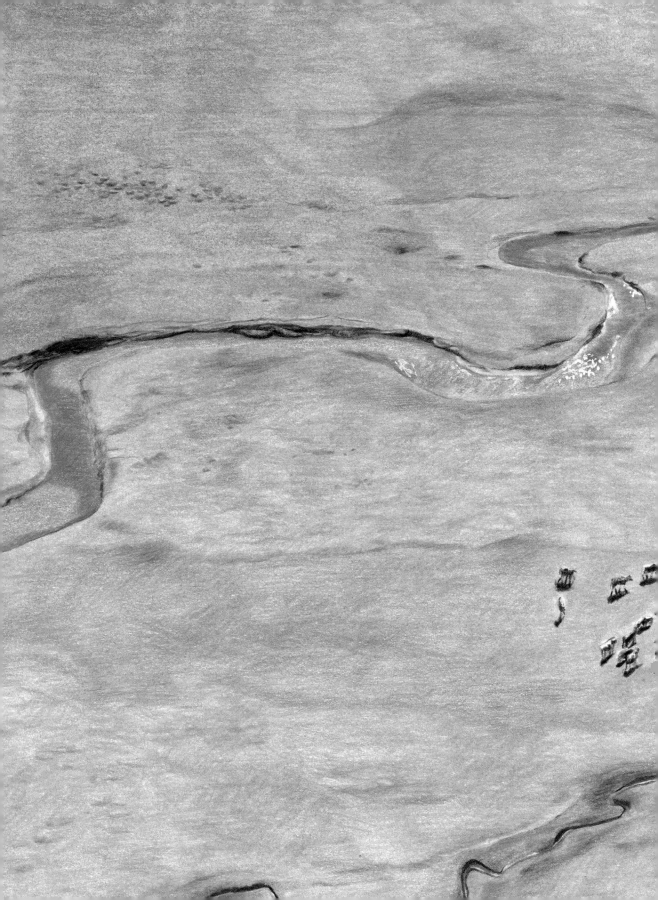

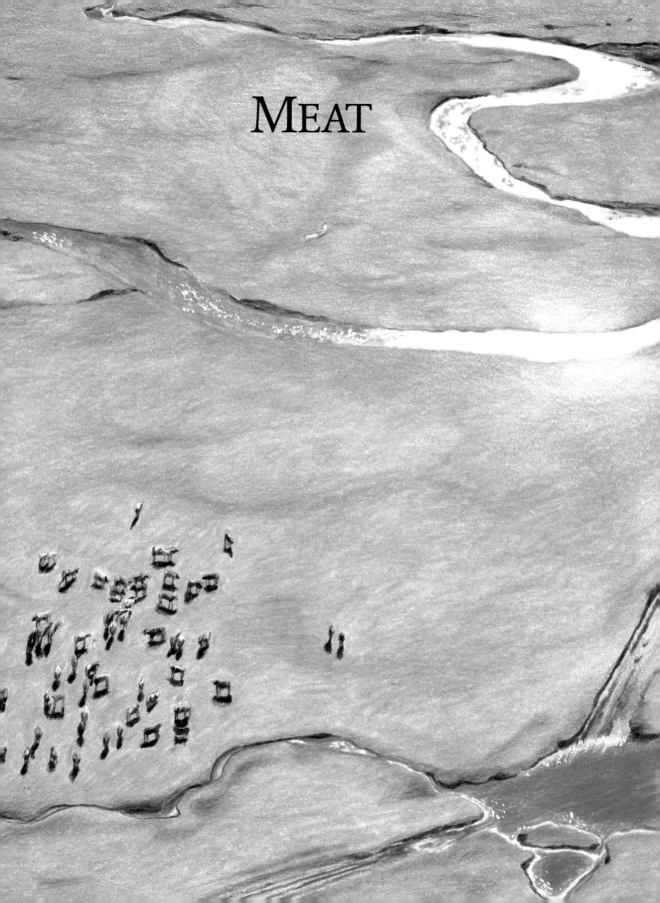

MEAT

MEAT

PORK IS THE most versatile and widely used meat in China. We Chinese do not have as great a preference for lean meat as you have in the West. Indeed, the top cut of pork in China is Five Flower Pork, the pork belly, which consists of skin and alternating layers of lean pork and fat. Although Westerners are horrified by the cholesterol levels of such cuts of pork, we Chinese eat very small quantities so that it isn't a problem.

Pork skin plays an important part in Chinese cooking. It is used in boiled and stewed dishes to thicken the stock or gravy, so that thickening agents (cornflour/cornstarch, potato flour, etc.) aren't necessary. This results in a very tasty sauce, which is useful for adding to rice and noodles, and for coating and flavouring vegetables.

Beef makes only an occasional appearance on the Chinese dining table, probably because cattle in China are raised as work animals rather than as a food source. In the areas south of the Yangzi (Yangtze) River, lamb is seldom eaten as it is considered a kind of game meat, which is not to the taste of the southern palates.

However, to the north nearer the steppes of the great grasslands of Mongolia and western Manchuria, large herds of cattle roam. Here lamb and beef are the principal meats. Lamb is popular as it doesn't require the lengthy cooking that tougher beef needs. Indeed, Beijing (Peking) was at one time gaining a reputation as "Mutton City", as many of its best known and most popular dishes contained lamb.

Many Chinese beef and lamb dishes have a Muslim/ Mongolian background and can now be eaten in Chinese Muslim restaurants in any principal city of China.

WHITE CUT GARLIC PORK
Bai Qiu Rou

1.25-1.5 kg (2½-3 lb) pork belly
  (cut to include several layers of
  lean and fat, in addition to a
  good layer of skin at the top)
4-5 slices root ginger
Salt, to taste
2.2-2.8 L (4-5 pt) water

DIP SAUCE

5-6 cloves garlic, crushed
3 tablespoons light soya sauce
4 tablespoons wine vinegar

4-6 portions with other dishes

THIS NORTHERN DISH is a good introductory course to a meal with a number of elaborately flavoured dishes.

Method: Place pork in a deep saucepan. Add ginger, salt and enough water to submerge the pork. Bring contents to the boil and boil for 10 minutes. Pour away one-third of the water. Reduce heat to a slow simmer, and simmer gently for 35 minutes, turning the pork over every 10 minutes.

To make the dip sauce, combine ingredients in a jug and divide between 2 small dip sauce dishes on the table.

Each tender slice of pork, should be first dipped into the sauce before it is eaten with hot rice. The uncomplicated flavours of the pork and rice make this an appealing dish.

Serving: Remove the pork from the pan and allow it to cool. When cold, cut the pork through the skin and the layers of lean and fat into slices 4 x 6 cm (1½-2½ in). Overlap them neatly on a serving plate.

BASIC RED-COOKED PORK

Hong Shao Rou

1.5-2 kg (3-4 lb) pork belly
3-4 slices root ginger
5-6 tablespoons dark soya sauce
3 teaspoons sugar

6-7 portions with other dishes

THIS PARTICULAR RECIPE is probably the most widely cooked meat dish in China. No doubt it is popular because it is easy to cook and is delicious with rice, noodles, steamed bread and vegetables.

Method: Cut pork into 1.5 x 6 x 4 cm (½ x 2½ x 1½ in) pieces each including skin and layers of lean and fat. Place the pork pieces in a pan of boiling water to boil for 5 minutes. Pour away three-quarters of the water, leaving sufficient to cover all the pork pieces.

Add ginger, soya sauce and sugar to the pan, sprinkling them evenly over the pork. Cover the pan firmly and bring to the boil. Lower the heat to the minimum and simmer as gently as possible for 1 hour and 15 minutes, turning the meat over every 15 minutes, and replenishing with 5-6 tablespoons of boiling water whenever the contents appear too dry.

If the pork is cooked in a casserole it can be placed into a preheated oven 195°C (390°F/Gas mark 6) and cooked for the same length of time, turning the meat over 3 times in the course of the cooking.

Serving: If the pork is cooked in a casserole it can be brought to the table for the diners to help themselves. The jelly-like tenderness of the meat and tastiness of the gravy make this dish particularly appealing.

Note: Basic Red-Cooked Pork can be varied into Red-Cooked Pork with Bamboo Shoots, or Red-Cooked Pork with Chestnuts simply by adding these additional items to the pan or casserole during the last 30 minutes of cooking.

RED-COOKED KNUCKLE OF PORK WITH SPINACH

Hong Shao Zhu Shou

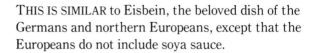

2 kg (4 lb) large knuckle of pork
Salt, to taste
4-5 tablespoons dark soya sauce
2 shallots (spring onions/scallions)
3 cloves garlic, crushed
3 slices root ginger
5 tablespoons vegetable oil
500 g (1 lb) fresh spinach
1 tablespoon sugar
3 tablespoon dry sherry
2 teaspoons red fermented tofu
*   (beancurd) cheese (optional)*

6-8 portions for a small party or
*   family gathering with other*
*   dishes*

THIS IS SIMILAR to Eisbein, the beloved dish of the Germans and northern Europeans, except that the Europeans do not include soya sauce.

Method: Clean the skin of the pork, removing any hair. Cut the knuckle-end half way lengthwise and remove the bone (or ask the butcher to do it). Rub the pork with salt and 2 tablespoons soya sauce. Cut shallots diagonally into 2.5 cm (1 in) sections and combine with garlic and ginger. Mix them all in a bowl with half of the remaining soya sauce.

Heat oil in a wok or frying pan. Add knuckle and fry for 7-8 minutes until slightly brown. Stuff the cavity of the knuckle with the shallots, garlic, ginger and soya sauce. Wash spinach thoroughly and drain.

Choose a deep casserole or heavy, heatproof pot with lid. Place the stuffed knuckle in it sitting vertically. Sprinkle with sugar, sherry, and the remainder of soya sauce and add the fermented tofu. Pour in sufficient water to cover the knuckle. Bring contents to boil and then transfer the casserole to the oven preheated to 200°C (400°F/Gas mark 6). After 15 minutes reduce heat to 180°C (350°F/Gas mark 4) and simmer very gently for 2½ hours, turning the knuckle over every 30 minutes. Lift the knuckle out to stand vertically at the centre of a large serving dish. Add the spinach to the casserole to cook over high heat for 6-7 minutes. Ladle out the sauce to surround the knuckle and pour what remaining gravy there is in the casserole over the top.

LION'S HEAD MEATBALLS

Shi Zi Tou

4 medium Chinese dried
　mushrooms
100 g (4 oz) Chinese transparent
　pea starch noodles
1.25 kg (2½ lb) pork belly (to
　include lean, fat and skin)
2 medium onions
4-5 medium water chestnuts
Salt, to taste
Pepper, to taste
2 tablespoons dark soya sauce
1½ teaspoons sugar
½ eggwhite, lightly beaten
Oil for deep-frying
5-6 teaspoons dark soya sauce extra
300 mL (½ pt) stock
2 shallots (spring onions/scallions),
　chopped

6-7 portions with other dishes

LION'S HEAD MEATBALLS are large party meal meatballs, which are so-called because the golden-brown noodles in the sauce resemble the mane of a lion. They are cooked for a long time to achieve succulence and tenderness.

Method: Soak dried mushrooms in boiling water for 30 minutes. Discard stems and chop caps finely. Soak transparent noodles in boiling water for 5-6 minutes and drain.

Chop and reduce pork into coarse mince with a cleaver or blender. Coarsely chop onions and water chestnuts. Place them in a bowl with salt, pepper, soya sauce, sugar and eggwhite. Mix together until well blended. Wet your fingers and palm so that the mince meat will not stick to them and form mixture into 5-6 large meatballs.

Heat oil in a wok or deep-fryer. When hot, add 2 meatballs at a time to fry lightly for 5 minutes or until slightly brown. Remove and arrange the meatballs at the bottom of a saucepan or heatproof bowl with a lid, suitable for putting in a steamer for lengthy steaming. Sprinkle the top of each meatball with 1 teaspoon soya sauce. Insert the bowl into a steamer and steam steadily for 2½ hours.

Serving: Remove and transfer the meatballs to a serving bowl. Pour the remaining liquid from the heatproof bowl into a saucepan. Add stock, chopped dried mushrooms, adjust for seasoning, and bring to boil for 5 minutes. Add the noodles to simmer together until cooked. Pour all the contents over the meatballs in the serving dish. Sprinkle with chopped shallots, and serve.

DOUBLE-COOKED PORK (TWICE-COOKED PORK)

Hui Guo Rou

1 kg (2¼ lb) pork belly
1 red capsicum (sweet pepper)
1 green capsicum (sweet pepper)
4 tablespoons vegetable oil
3 cloves garlic, chopped
60 g (2 oz) Sichuan Zha Cai
    pickles, chopped
2 chillies (hot peppers) chopped
2 tablespoons dry sherry
1½ tablespoons shallots (spring
    onions/scallions), coarsely
    chopped
1 teaspoon sesame oil

SAUCE

1½ tablespoons yellow bean paste
2 tablespoons dark soya sauce
2 tablespoons tomato purée
1½ tablespoons Hai Xian (Hoisin)
    sauce
2 teaspoons chilli sauce
2 tablespoons stock

5-6 portions with other dishes

THIS IS A SPICY dish, which is fairly typical of the flavour of Sichuan food.

Method: Boil pork in ample water for 35 minutes. When cold, drain and cut into 1 x 6 x 4 cm (¼ x 2½ x 1½ in) lean-and-fat rectangular slices. Remove seeds from capsicums and cut into 4 cm (1½ in) strips. To make the sauce, mix the ingredients until well blended.

Heat the oil in a wok or frying pan. When hot, add the garlic, pickles and chillies, and stir them in the hot oil for 30 seconds. Pour in the sauce and heat until it bubbles over high heat. Add the sliced pork and spread out to turn in the sauce. Continue to stir-fry over high heat for 2 full minutes. Sprinkle with sherry, shallots and sesame oil, stir and serve.

PORK SPARE RIBS

Men Kao Pai Gu

1.75-2 kg (3½-4 lb) pork spare ribs
Salt, to taste
Pepper, to taste
600 mL (1 pt) strong stock

MARINADE

2 tablespoons fermented salted
  black beans, chopped and
  mashed
2 tablespoons light soya sauce
1 tablespoon yellow bean paste
4 slices root ginger, finely chopped
3 cloves garlic, crushed
1 medium onion, sliced
1 tablespoon sugar
3 tablespoons dry sherry
2 tablespoons vegetable oil

5-6 portions

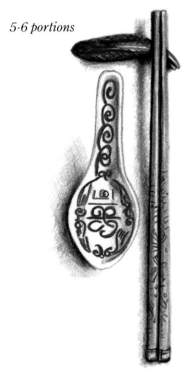

SPARE RIBS HAVE now become a universally popular dish that probably originated in China. One of the first jobs in cooking spare ribs is to render the meat sufficiently tender so that it can be easily detached from the bone. This tenderising process is achieved by stewing or steaming. If they are steamed, the ribs need to be marinated in advance. The flavour can be further enhanced by next crisping the spare ribs for a short period by deep-frying or roasting in a hot oven.

In the average Western kitchen the simplest process of cooking spare ribs is to stew them first, then crisp them in a hot oven.

Method: Cut spare ribs into individual ribs. Rub them evenly with salt, and pepper to taste. Mix all the ingredients for the marinade in a large bowl. Add the spare ribs. Turn and rub the ribs with the marinade several times until every rib is well coated. Refrigerate and leave them to stand for 30 minutes.

Heat stock in a large casserole. Add the ribs, and spread them evenly into the boiling stock. Pour in any remainder of marinade. Cover the casserole, reduce heat and simmer for 30-35 minutes, turning the ribs over every 10-12 minutes. Remove the lid from the casserole and place in an oven preheated to 200°C (400°F/Gas mark 6). Roast for approximately 10-12 minutes, when the ribs should be encrusted with the marinade, and ready to serve.

Serving: Serve by bringing the casserole to the table for the diners to help themselves. As spare ribs are an informal dish, diners are encouraged to use their fingers.

SWEET AND SOUR PORK

Gu Lu Rou

500 g (1 lb) leg of pork
Salt, to taste
½ eggwhite, lightly beaten
1½ tablespoons cornflour
   (cornstarch)
1 medium red or green capsicum
   (sweet pepper)
5 tablespoons vegetable oil
1 medium onion, thinly sliced
1 slice pineapple, cubed

SAUCE

1 tablespoon cornflour (cornstarch)
2 tablespoons water
3½ tablespoons wine vinegar
1 tablespoon light soya sauce
1½ tablespoons sugar
2 tablespoons orange juice
1 tablespoon tomato purée

6-7 portions with other dishes

THE APPEAL OF this dish, which is probably similar to that of the French dish *Duck à l'Orange*, is the way it sets off the richness of the meat with the freshness of the slightly sharp fruity sauce.

Method: Cut pork into thick slices, and then roughly into 4 x 2.5 cm (1½ x 1 in) pieces. Rub with salt, wet with eggwhite and dredge with cornflour. Cut capsicum into 4 cm (1½ in) strips. To make the sauce, mix the ingredients together until well blended.

Heat oil in a wok or a frying pan. When hot, add the pork pieces and stir-fry over medium heat for 3 minutes. Remove them with a perforated spoon and set aside.

Drain away half of the remaining oil. Add the onion and stir-fry for 1 minute. Add the pineapple and capsicum. Continue to stir-fry for another minute. Pour in the sauce and stir until the sauce thickens. Return the pork pieces to the wok and mix with the sauce over medium heat for 1½ minutes, or until every piece of pork appears glistening and well coated with the sauce. Serve with rice.

CANTONESE CHA SHAO BARBECUE PORK

Chao Shao

1 kg (2 lb) fillet of pork

MARINADE

3 tablespoons dark soya sauce
1½ tablespoons Hai Xian (Hoisin)
  sauce
1½ tablespoons yellow bean paste
1 tablespoon sugar
1½ tablespoons tomato purée
1 tablespoon dry sherry
1 tablespoon vegetable oil

6-7 portions with other dishes

THE APPEAL OF this dish lies in the rim of rich encrustation which surrounds each piece of pork, while inside the meat is very moist and juicy. It can be eaten hot or cold. When served cold, it can be used as an appetizer.

Method: Clean the pork thoroughly, removing any fat or membrane. To make the marinade, mix all the ingredients together until well blended and pour over the entire fillet of pork, rubbing it into the meat thoroughly. Refrigerate and leave pork to stand in the marinade for a couple of hours, basting and turning the meat over every 30 minutes.

Pre-heat the oven to 200°C (400°F/Gas mark 6). Place the pork in a roasting pan and bake for 20-25 minutes, turning the pork over after the first 10 minutes. Cut the pork on a chopping board across the grain into 1 cm (¼ in) thick slices.

Serving: Serve the pork by overlapping the slices on a serving plate.

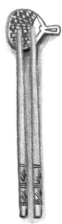

RED-COOKED FIVE SPICE BEEF WITH TURNIP
Luo Bo Men Niu Nan

1.25 kg (2½ lb) shin beef
500 g (1 lb) turnips
3½ tablespoons vegetable oil
2 medium onions, thinly sliced
3 slices root ginger, shredded
¾ teaspoon five spice powder
Salt, to taste
900 mL (1½ pt) water
3½ tablespoons dark soya sauce
2 teaspoons sugar
6 tablespoons rice wine or dry
    sherry

6-7 portions with other dishes

THIS IS A VERY tasty dish, excellent to consume on a cold wintry day!

Method: Boil beef for 10 minutes and cut into 4 x 2.5 cm (1½ x 1 in) cubes. Clean and cut turnips diagonally into 4 cm (1½ in) pieces.

Heat oil in a casserole or heavy pan. When hot, add beef and stir-fry the beef cubes for 3-4 minutes. Remove with perforated spoon and set aside. Add onions, ginger, five spice and salt. Stir-fry for 3-4 minutes. Pour in water. Add soya sauce, sugar, wine or sherry. Bring contents to the boil. Add the beef cubes. When contents return to the boil, reduce heat to a minimum, cover and simmer very gently for 1½ hours. Add the turnips and turn the contents over several times. Add 300 mL (½ pt) of water if the contents begin to run too dry. Turn the contents over again. Cover the casserole and place in an oven preheated to 195°C (390°F/Gas mark 6) for a further 1¾ hours.

Serving: Bring the casserole to the table. Remove the lid, and allow diners to help themselves, spooning the beef, turnips and gravy into their own bowl with rice.

RED-COOKED LAMB WITH CARROTS AND DRIED TANGERINE PEEL

Chen Pi Yang Rou

1.25 kg (2½ lb) leg of lamb
500 g (1 lb) carrots
3½ tablespoons vegetable oil
2 medium onions
3 slices root ginger
3 cloves garlic, crushed
2½ tablespoons dried tangerine
   peel, in small pieces
Salt, to taste
900 mL (1½ pt) water
3½ teaspoons dark soya sauce
1 teaspoon sugar
6 tablespoons rice wine or dry
   sherry

6-7 portions with other dishes

THIS LAMB DISH is very similar to Red-Cooked Five Spice Beef with Turnip, except that here, the turnips are replaced by carrots, and the five spice powder by dried tangerine peel, which is used frequently for flavouring in long-cooked meat dishes. Since leg of lamb can be tenderised much more quickly than shin of beef, the overall cooking time can be shortened by one hour.

Method: Boil the lamb and cut into 4 x 2.5 cm (1½ x 1 in) cubes. Clean and cut the carrots diagonally into 4 cm (1½ in) sections.

Heat oil in a casserole. When hot, add lamb and stir-fry for 3-4 minutes. Remove with a perforated spoon and set aside. Add onions, ginger, garlic, tangerine peel and salt. Stir-fry for 3-4 minutes. Pour in water and add soya sauce, sugar, wine or sherry. Bring to the boil and add the lamb cubes. Reduce heat to low, cover and simmer gently. The carrots should be added to the pot after the lamb has been cooking for 1 hour. Stir contents and cover. Place casserole in the oven preheated to 195°C (390°F/Gas mark 6) for another hour. It is then ready to serve.

SLICED BEEF IN SOFT SCRAMBLED EGGS

Niu Rou Chao Dan

500 g (1 lb) fillet of beef
Salt, to taste
Pepper, to taste
3 eggs, beaten
1 tablespoon shallots (spring
onions/scallions)
½ tablespoon Hai Xian (Hoisin)
sauce
3 tablespoons vegetable oil
1 tablespoon dry sherry

MARINADE

1½ tablespoons dark soya sauce
½ tablespoon yellow bean paste
½ tablespoon Hai Xian (Hoisin)
sauce
1 teaspoon chilli sauce

4-5 portions with other dishes

THE AROMA OF wine combines well with the taste of eggs, giving this dish an interesting flavour.

Method: Cut beef into very thin slices 5 x 4 cm (2 x 1½ in) in size. Place them in a bowl. Mix all the marinade ingredients together until well blended. Add the marinade to the beef and rub it into every individual slice of beef. Refrigerate and leave to season for 30 minutes. Add seasonings to beaten eggs with chopped shallots, Hai Xian sauce and 1 tablespoon of oil. Beat again for another ¼ minute.

Heat half the remaining oil (1 tablespoon) in a wok or frying pan. When hot, arrange the sliced beef spread out in a single layer to shallow-fry for 45 seconds, over medium heat. Stir-fry them for another ½ minute. Remove them and set aside. Add the remaining 1 tablespoon of oil. Tilt the wok so that the oil evenly covers the surface. Pour in the beaten egg. When it is half set and still wet on the top, add the slices of beef to scramble and stir-fry together with the egg. Sprinkle with sherry, stir and turn over medium heat.

Serving: This is an excellent dish to eat hot with plain rice.

COLD-TOSSED BEEF IN MUSTARD SAUCE WITH FRESH CORIANDER

Liang Ban Niu Rou

700 g (1½ lb) fillet or rump steak
Salt, to taste
Pepper, to taste
1 tablespoon vegetable oil
1 small bunch coriander leaves,
  washed
1½ tablespoons rice wine or dry
  sherry

SAUCE

3 teaspoons English mustard
1½ tablespoons light soya sauce
1 tablespoon vinegar
1½ tablespoons stock
1 tablespoon sesame oil

8-12 portions as a starter

THIS IS A VERY useful dish to serve as an appetizer.

Method: Boil beef in a panful of water for 15 minutes. When cold, cut into very thin slices approximately 6 x 2.5 cm (2½ x 1 in) in size. Rub beef with salt, pepper and oil. To make the sauce, mix the ingredients together until well blended.

Serving: Mix and toss the beef and the sauce together, in a large deep-sided serving bowl. Strew the top with sprays of coriander leaves, wine or sherry. Mix and toss them together once more and serve.

SICHUAN SHREDDED BEEF WITH CARROTS AND CELERY

Si Chuan Niu Rou Si

500 g (1 lb) rump steak
Salt, to taste
4 tablespoons cornflour
  (cornstarch)
1 egg, beaten
2 slices root ginger
2 medium carrots
2-3 sticks celery
Oil for deep-frying
2 tablespoons stock

SAUCE

1½ tablespoons cornflour
  (cornstarch), blended with 3
  tablespoons water
1 tablespoon light soya sauce
1 tablespoon sugar
2 tablespoons vinegar
2 tablespoons rice wine
¾ tablespoon Sichuan Dou Ban
  (Toupan) chilli and soya sauce

6-8 portions with other dishes

THE HOT SPICINESS of the sweet and sour sauce here gives this dish its typical Sichuan character and appeal.

Method: Cut the beef into double matchsticks. Rub with salt. Mix cornflour with beaten egg to blend to a smooth batter. Coat beef with a layer of batter. Clean and cut ginger, carrots and celery into the same size matchsticks as the beef. To make the sauce, mix the ingredients together until well blended.

Heat the oil in a wok. When hot (a crumb will sizzle when dropped into it), add the beef slowly, in small quantities. Use a fork or a pair of chopsticks to keep the shredded beef apart, so that they will fry singly rather than in large clusters. Continue to stir with the chopsticks. After 3-3½ minutes frying over medium heat, remove and drain the beef and put aside. Pour away most of the oil.

Add the shredded carrots, celery and ginger and stir in the remaining oil in the wok for 1 minute. Add stock and stir once more. Pour in the sauce. Turn the heat to high. When the contents begin to boil, return the shredded beef to the wok and stir in the sauce with the vegetables. Stir-fry for 1 minute and serve.

BEEF IN OYSTER SAUCE WITH SNOW PEAS (MANGE TOUT)

He Dou Niu Rou

500 g (1 lb) beef steak
Salt, to taste
Pepper, to taste
1 eggwhite, lightly beaten
2 tablespoons cornflour
(cornstarch)
120-150 g (4-5 oz) snow peas
(mange tout)
4 tablespoons vegetable oil
2 slices root ginger, coarsely
chopped
2¼ tablespoons oyster sauce
3 tablespoons stock
1½ tablespoons wine or sherry
1½ tablespoons dark soya sauce

5-6 portions with other dishes

THIS IS A TYPICAL Cantonese dish with an interesting blend of beef and oyster flavours.

Method: Cut beef into thin slices 5 x 4 cm (2 x 1½ in) in size. Rub with salt and pepper to taste, wet with eggwhite and dredge with cornflour. Poach snow peas in boiling water for 1 minute and drain.

Heat oil in a wok or frying pan. When hot, add the ginger to flavour the oil, and spread out beef in the wok. Add half of the oyster sauce to the beef, stir-fry for 1 minute, remove and set aside. Add the snow peas to the wok, then the stock and wine or sherry. Turn the heat to high to stir-fry the vegetables for 1 minute. Return the beef to the wok, sprinkle the contents with the soya sauce and the remaining oyster sauce, stir and mix the contents for a further 1 minute and serve.

Serving: This dish is normally served with rice, but it may also be served as a savoury starter.

BEEF IN BLACK BEAN SAUCE WITH CAPSICUMS (SWEET PEPPERS)

Chi Jiao Niu Rou

500 g (1 lb) rump steak
1 eggwhite, lightly beaten
2 tablespoons cornflour
  (cornstarch)
2 medium green or red capsicums
  (sweet peppers), seeded
1½ tablespoons salted black beans
3 tablespoons vegetable oil
1 tablespoon dark soya sauce
1 tablespoon stock
1 tablespoon rice wine or dry
  sherry
½ tablespoon Sichuan Dou Ban
  (Toupan) chilli and soya sauce

5 portions with other dishes

THIS DISH should be served with ample rice.

Method: Cut beef into thin slices 5 x 2.5 cm (2 x 1 in) in size. Wet with eggwhite and dredge with cornflour. Cut capsicums into 5 x 2.5 cm (2 x 1 in) strips. Soak black beans in hot water for 20 minutes, and drain, leaving 1½ tablespoons water with the beans.

Heat oil in a wok or frying pan. When hot, add the beef and stir-fry over medium heat for 1¼ minutes. Remove beef and set aside. Add black beans with water and mash with the oil in the wok. Return the beef to the wok to coat with a layer of the sauce. Add soya sauce, stock, wine or sherry, Sichuan Dou Ban paste and the capsicums. Stir-fry together for 1 minute over high heat and serve.

PEPPERED BEEF WITH ONION

Hei Jiao Niu Liu

500 g (1 lb) fillet of beef
Salt, to taste
Pepper, to taste
1 eggwhite, lightly beaten
2 tablespoons cornflour
   (cornstarch)
5 tablespoons vegetable oil
2 slices root ginger, coarsely
   chopped
1 teaspoon Sichuan peppercorns
2 medium onions, thinly sliced
1½ teaspoons sugar
2 tablespoons dark soya sauce

5-6 portions with other dishes

THE PEPPERED BEEF in this dish is popular in the West.

Method: Cut beef into thin slices 5 x 4 cm (2 x 1½ in) in size. Rub with salt and a generous sprinkle of pepper, wet with eggwhite and dredge in cornflour.

Heat 4 tablespoons oil in wok or frying pan. When hot, add ginger and peppercorns. Stir-fry over medium heat for 45 seconds. Add the beef, spreading it out over the wok and stir-fry for 1 minute over high heat. Remove and set aside.

Add remaining oil, and when hot, add the sliced onions. Stir-fry for 1½ minutes. Add sugar and soya sauce, return the beef, continue to stir-fry all the ingredients for 1½ minutes over high heat and serve.

Serving: This is a dish which should be served hot with rice.

PEKING SLICED LAMB MONGOLIAN HOT POT

Shuan Yang Rou

TABLE DIPS; *the following mixture of ingredients may be tried*

DIP 1
slices of root ginger, shredded,
3 tablespoons light soya sauce,
5 tablespoons wine vinegar,
1 tablespoon vegetable oil.

DIP 2
5 cloves garlic (crushed),
3 tablespoons light soya sauce,
2 tablespoons wine vinegar,
2 tablespoons dry sherry,
1 tablespoon sesame oil.

DIP 3
3 shallots (spring onions/scallions),
  coarsely chopped,
3 tablespoons light soya sauce,
2 tablespoons tomato sauce,
1½ tablespoons Sichuan chilli
  paste,
1 tablespoon sesame oil.

DIP 4
3 tablespoons chopped coriander
  leaves,
1½ tablespoons English mustard,
2 tablespoons light soya sauce,
2 tablespoons stock,
1 tablespoon vegetable oil,
1½ tablespoons dry sherry,
1 tablespoon sesame oil.

THIS DISH IS one of the best known culinary features of Beijing (Peking) and was first introduced from Mongolia in 1855 during the reign of Emperor Shanfeng of the Qing Dynasty. Traditionally only lamb was used, but as the dish became popular further south, other types of meat, such as chicken, beef and pork, were added. Later, even fish and seafood were cooked in this way.

The original recipe, of several thousand words, took a whole chapter of a book to describe the preparation, cooking and consumption of the dish. Yet, in reality, it is such a simple dish that it should not take more than half a postcard to describe and present. Here, I shall describe and present it as simply and concisely as I can.

Having had this dish scores of times during the five years I spent in Beijing I would say that the dish consists of nothing more than a leg of lamb cut into extremely thin slices. The slices are then spread out on serving dishes in single sheet layers for diners to help themselves. There should be at least two dishfuls of lamb for each diner.

The dish is sometimes called *Fondue Chinois*. As with Swiss fondue the diners actually do the cooking at the dining table. In Beijing, the cooking is usually done in a hotpot fired by charcoal fire. In the West it can be done in any deep-sided heavy pot in which the heat can be easily controlled.

The main purpose of the cooking is simply to dip the extremely thinly sliced lamb in the boiling broth for not more than 1 minute. It is then immediately withdrawn with a pair of chopsticks and dipped into one of the dip-sauces provided on the dining table.

DIP 5
*3 tablespoons sesame paste (or
    peanut butter),*
2 tablespoons light soya sauce.

*5-6 portions for a family
    gathering or group of friends*

Once it has been dipped in the sauce, it can be eaten. These dip-sauces play an important role in giving flavour and character to the dish.

With the array of dip-sauces there should be a good range of alternative concoctions for the diners to choose from.

The boiler for cooking should be deep and big enough to hold 2 L (3½ pt) of stock and to keep it at a rolling boil. The stock is used up quite rapidly, and at least another 1.2 L (2 pt) of stock should be kept in reserve for immediate replenishment as soon as the liquid in the boiler begins to run low. Twelve platefuls of sliced lamb should not last more than ¾ hour of continuous cooking by the diners. When all the meat has been cooked, the stock in the boiler should be rich and savoury. Add 500 g (1 lb) of Chinese white cabbage (also called Chinese leaves), which has been thoroughly cleaned and cut into 5 cm (2 in) length segments, to the broth in the boiler. Cover with a lid, bring to a gentle boil, and lower the heat to simmer. Simmer for 8-10 minutes. The lid can then be removed and the soup ladled out into the individual bowls of the diners and drunk as a hot refreshing wash down!

This is a very warming experience on a winter's evening and you don't even have to venture as far as Mongolia or Beijing!

SLICED LAMB WITH LEEK AND GARLIC

Dai Suan Yang Rou Pian

1 kg (2¼ lb) leg of lamb
Salt, to taste
1 eggwhite, lightly beaten
2 tablespoons cornflour
    (cornstarch)
375 g (¾ lb) young leeks
4 tablespoons vegetable oil
4 slices root ginger, shredded
1 medium onion, thinly sliced
5 cloves garlic, crushed
3 tablespoons dark soya sauce
4 tablespoons stock

5-6 portions

THE LAMB DISH I remember best from Beijing
(Peking) was the one I always encountered when
I entered the rickshaw-pullers' eating hut to obtain a
ride in the winters of the 1930s. As soon as I lifted
the heavily padded curtain to enter the hut, I was
greeted and nearly thrown back by the overpowering
smell of garlic. The dish which was being cooked was
Sliced Lamb with Leek and Garlic.

Method: Cut lamb with a sharp knife into thin slices
5 x 4 cm (2 x 1½ in) in size. Rub with salt, wet with
eggwhite and dredge in cornflour. Clean leeks
thoroughly and cut diagonally into 5 cm (2 in)
sections.
   Heat the oil in a wok or a large frying pan. When
hot, add the ginger and onion, and stir-fry over high
heat for 1 minute. Add the garlic and lamb. Continue
to stir and turn all the contents in the wok over high
heat for 2 minutes. Push away from the centre of the
heat. Add the leeks and stir-fry them for 1 minute
over medium heat. Pour the soya sauce and stock
over them. Turn and stir the vegetables in the
bubbling sauce for 45 seconds. Now bring the lamb
back to mix and turn with the leeks over high heat
for 2 minutes.

Serving: Serve on a well-heated serving plate for the
diners to help themselves.

INDEX